THE SERMON ON THE MOUNT

The Pro Ecclesia Series

Books in the Pro Ecclesia series are "for the Church." The series is sponsored by the Center for Catholic and Evangelical Theology, founded by Carl Braaten and Robert Jenson in 1991. The series seeks to nourish the Church's faithfulness to the gospel of Jesus Christ through a theology that is self-critically committed to the biblical, dogmatic, liturgical, and ethical traditions that form the foundation for a fruitful ecumenical theology. The series reflects a commitment to the classical tradition of the Church as providing the resources critically needed by the various churches as they face modern and post-modern challenges. The series will include books by individuals as well as collections of essays by individuals and groups. The Editorial Board will be drawn from various Christian traditions.

TITLES IN THE SERIES INCLUDE:

The Morally Divided Body: Ethical Disagreement and the Unity of the Church, edited by Michael Root and James J. Buckley

Christian Theology and Islam, edited by Michael Root and James J. Buckley

Who Do You Say That I Am?: Proclaiming and Following Jesus Today, edited by Michael Root and James J. Buckley

What Does It Mean to "Do This"?: Supper, Mass, Eucharist, edited by Michael Root and James J. Buckley

Heaven, Hell, . . . and Purgatory?, edited by Michael Root and James J. Buckley

Life Amid the Principalities: Identifying, Understanding, and Engaging Created, Fallen, and Disarmed Powers Today, edited by Michael Root and James J. Buckley

Remembering the Reformation: Commemorate? Celebrate? Repent?, edited by Michael Root and James J. Buckley

The Emerging Christian Minority, edited by Victor Lee Austin and Joel C. Daniels

Repentance and Forgiveness, edited by Matthew E. Burdette and Victor Lee Austin

What's the Good of Humanity?, edited by Victor Lee Austin and Joel C. Daniels

Hope Today, edited by Matthew E. Burdette and Victor Lee Austin

Mixed Blessings: The Theologians Who Shaped Us, edited by Victor Lee Austin

The Sermon on the Mount

Reflections for the Church

Edited by
Victor Lee Austin

CASCADE *Books* • Eugene, Oregon

THE SERMON ON THE MOUNT
Reflections for the Church

The Pro Ecclesia Series 13

Copyright © 2025 Wipf and Stock Publishers. All rights reserved. Except for brief quotations in critical publications or reviews, no part of this book may be reproduced in any manner without prior written permission from the publisher. Write: Permissions, Wipf and Stock Publishers, 199 W. 8th Ave., Suite 3, Eugene, OR 97401.

Cascade Books
An Imprint of Wipf and Stock Publishers
199 W. 8th Ave., Suite 3
Eugene, OR 97401

www.wipfandstock.com

PAPERBACK ISBN: 979-8-3852-3054-9
HARDCOVER ISBN: 979-8-3852-3055-6
EBOOK ISBN: 979-8-3852-3056-3

Cataloguing-in-Publication data:

Names: Austin, Victor Lee, editor.

Title: The Sermon on the mount : reflections for the church / edited by Victor Lee Austin.

Description: Eugene, OR : Cascade Books, 2025 | Series: Pro Ecclesia Series 13

Identifiers: ISBN 979-8-3852-3054-9 (paperback) | ISBN 979-8-3852-3055-6 (hardcover) | ISBN 979-8-3852-3056-3 (ebook)

Subjects: LCSH: Sermon on the mount.

Classification: BT380.2 .S45 2025 (paperback) | BT380.2 .S45 (ebook)

VERSION NUMBER 03/05/25

Scripture quotations not otherwise attributed are from the New Revised Standard Version Bible, copyright © 1989 National Council of the Churches of Christ in the United States of America. Used by permission. All rights reserved worldwide.

The editor gratefully acknowledges permission to reprint Sarah Hinlicky Wilson, *Sermon on the Mount: A Poetic Paraphrase* (St. Paul: Thornbush, 2020).

Contents

Contributors vii

Editor's Preface ix
VICTOR LEE AUSTIN

1. The Sermon on the Mount in Matthew's Gospel 1
   MARIANNE MEYE THOMPSON

2. The Sermon on the Mount as Law and Gospel 18
   PIOTR J. MAŁYSZ

3. Reading the Sermon on the Mount in a Culture of Victimhood 33
   DAVID CLOUTIER

4. Is the Sermon on the Mount Economically Realistic? 54
   BRENT WATERS

5. Preaching the Sermon on the Mount 69
   SARAH HINLICKY WILSON

   Special Supplement
   After the Ball Is Over: The Rise and Decline of the Ecumenical Movement 92
   MICHAEL ROOT

Contributors

Victor Lee Austin is Theologian-in-Residence for the Episcopal Diocese of Dallas and author of, among other books, *Friendship: The Heart of Being Human* and *A Post-COVID Catechesis* (Cascade).

David Cloutier is Professor of Theology at the University of Notre Dame, where he is also a fellow in the Business, Ethics, and Society Program at the Mendoza School of Business. He is the author of numerous books and articles, including *The Vice of Luxury: Economic Excess in a Consumer Age*.

Piotr J. Małysz is Associate Professor of Divinity at Beeson Divinity School, where he teaches the history of the Christian tradition. He is the author of *Trinity, Freedom, and Love: An Engagement with the Theology of Eberhard Jüngel*, as well as numerous articles on Luther and the Lutheran tradition. He serves as editor of *Lutheran Forum*.

Michael Root is Professor Emeritus of Systematic Theology at the Catholic University of America in Washington, DC. He is the author (with Bruce D. Marshall) of the forthcoming *Justification and Grace: Cross-Border Reflections* (Cascade).

Marianne Meye Thompson is the George Eldon Ladd Professor Emerita of New Testament at Fuller Theological Seminary. She is the author of *John: A Commentary*.

Brent Waters is the Emeritus Stead Professor of Christian Social Ethics, Garrett-Evangelical Theological Seminary. He is author of *Common Callings and Ordinary Virtues: Christian Ethics for Everyday Life*, among a few other books.

CONTRIBUTORS

Sarah Hinlicky Wilson is the author of *Seven Ways of Looking at the Transfiguration* and many other books. With Paul R. Hinlicky she co-hosts the podcast *Queen of the Sciences: Conversations Between a Theologian and Her Dad.*

Editor's Preface

JESUS' SERMON ON THE Mount marks a radical departure—on this, all can agree. It is high poetry, opening with the eight "beatitudes" that run from "Blessed are the poor in spirit: for theirs is the kingdom of heaven" through sorrow, meekness, the longing for righteousness, mercy, purity, peacemaking, to the concluding pronouncement that circles back to the first: "Blessed are they which are persecuted for righteousness' sake: for theirs is the kingdom of heaven."

Our Lord's teaching includes metaphor that calls for appropriate action: We are salt and light and should live accordingly. He claims not to be departing from his Hebrew heritage but to be taking it down to its very core. You have heard it said, for instance, "Thou shalt not kill," but he says, you shall not be angry. And so on, through a number of the Ten Commandments, all pointing to a summons to be like "your Father which is in heaven."

From poetry to high calling, Jesus aims repeatedly at our inmost parts, our heart. Pray in secret, for instance. Put your treasure in heaven—for then, your heart will be in heaven also. He aims to disabuse us of worldly anxiety, to attend to the birds of the air and the flowers of the field, all of which God takes care of.

But he also teaches about judgment, about being honest about ourselves (recognizing that log in our own eye). At the verbal center of the Sermon we find the inexhaustible treasure of the Lord's Prayer. And at the end, the memorable image of building a house. If we hear Jesus' words and do them, our house will be built on a rock. "And the rain descended, and the floods came, and the winds blew, and beat upon that house; and it fell not." But if we fail to do Jesus' words, our house is built on sand, and it will fall.

All this is beautiful and arresting. It is memorable, at least in its various parts. Yet it is also manifestly deep. Each verse of it is profound in itself.

Editor's Preface

And study of how its parts relate to each other also leads to profundities. No Christian who has ever existed has felt he or she completely understood the Sermon on the Mount. Every Christian who reads it again finds a new depth, a new insight, a new summons.

A depth, an insight, a summons—to what? That is the question. Is this about ethics, or about doctrine, or about perfection of life for a few people, or about everyday life for any Christian, or about spirituality, or about economics, or about poetry, or about mission? Yes to all these—and to many more.

This volume contains papers from scholars, from a range of ecclesial contexts, invited to address the Sermon from a number of directions. They hardly provide a final word, a complete, definitive understanding of this great teaching of our great Teacher. That is impossible. What they do provide is insight from different and complementary perspectives that can help the reader's mind and heart move within the Sermon. First, Marianne Meye Thompson grounds us in the actual text of the Sermon in the context of Matthew's Gospel. Piotr Małysz then leads us toward theological amazement at how the Sermon is at once law and gospel. The two following chapters help us see the Sermon as contemporaneous with ourselves. David Cloutier works with the Sermon to understand and critique our culture of victimhood, and Brent Waters goes back and forth on its economic "realism." Finally, Sarah Hinlicky Wilson takes us back to the text itself through her own poetic paraphrase and reflections on how preachers might actually address the Sermon as a whole.

This volume thus moves from exegesis to theology to application to proclamation. We offer it for the church (*pro ecclesia*) and in particular to our readers with the prayerful hope that they will come to a greater understanding and awe of this great text—and with that, greater awe and fuller worship of our Lord and Teacher.

The Center for Catholic and Evangelical Theology, which sponsors this Pro Ecclesia series, has had from its beginning a particular concern for doing theology ecumenically. At a recent conference, Michael Root, a seasoned ecumenical theologian and for a good decade executive director of CCET, set out to examine the changes in the ecumenical movement over the past generation or so. We are pleased to include his address as a special supplement to this volume.

Victor Lee Austin

1

The Sermon on the Mount in Matthew's Gospel

Marianne Meye Thompson

OUT OF MATTHEW'S TWENTY-EIGHT chapters, three have taken on a life of their own, and are commonly designated "the Sermon on the Mount." Countless books and articles have been devoted to their exposition as a stand-alone unit of text. There are critical commentaries, monographs, popular studies, and even bibliographies and histories of the interpretation of the Sermon.[1] Certain methods of studying the Gospels have allowed for, even commended, the treatment of this "sermon" as a separate entity, with attention given to its original setting, structure, purpose, and the like,

1. Among numerous studies, see Harvey K. McArthur, *Understanding the Sermon on the Mount* (London: Epworth, 1960); Robert A. Guelich, *The Sermon on the Mount: A Foundation for Understanding* (Waco: Word, 1982); Clarence Bauman, *The Sermon on the Mount: The Modern Quest for Its Meaning* (Macon, GA: Mercer University Press, 1985); Pinchas Lapide, *The Sermon on the Mount: Utopia or Program for Action?* (Maryknoll, NY: Orbis, 1986); Warren Carter, *What Are They Saying About Matthew and the Sermon on the Mount?* (New York: Paulist, 1994); Hans Dieter Betz, *The Sermon on the Mount: A Commentary on the Sermon on the Mount, Including the Sermon on the Plain (Matt 5:3-27 and Luke 6:20-49)*, Hermeneia (Minneapolis: Fortress, 1995); Dale C. Allison, *The Sermon on the Mount: Inspiring the Moral Imagination*, Companions to the New Testament (New York: Crossroad, 1999); Charles H. Talbert, *Reading the Sermon on the Mount: Character Formation and Decision Making in Matthew 5–7* (Grand Rapids: Baker Academic, 2006); Scot McKnight, *Sermon on the Mount*, The Story of God Bible Commentary (Grand Rapids: Zondervan, 2013).

almost as though it had existed and perhaps circulated prior to finding a place in Matthew's Gospel. To be sure, form criticism had posited that the smaller gospel traditions originally circulated as discrete units intended to meet various needs of early Christian communities. Eventually, these units were brought together as so many "pearls on a string" and combined to form the gospel narratives. But the form critics were more interested in the pearls than the string. They paid attention to parts, not to the whole, even as students of the Sermon have often paid attention to it as an entity quite apart from the Gospel of Matthew.

Perhaps because of the influence of such theories regarding gospel origins, most seminary students know that Matthew inserts "five discourses" into his narrative and that these discourses are marked, at the beginning and end, with a formulaic introduction and conclusion.[2] A short bit of verse I first heard in a seminary class makes the point:

> Matthew gives us five discourses;
> In threes and sevens he groups his sources.
> He writes to show what the OT meant,
> With an ecclesiastic bent.

It is not difficult to identify, label, and even extract, these five discourses from their contexts: here we have a chapter on the parables of the kingdom (ch. 13); there, a chapter on church discipline (ch. 18) or "the last things" (chs. 24–25). But the longest and most studied of the discourses is unquestionably the first: the Sermon on the Mount.

This so-called Sermon is set in the context of a narrative—as indeed are the other discourses. To understand and interpret any of these discourses properly requires that they be interpreted not only *within* their narrative context but as *part* of that narrative. Theologian Stanley Hauerwas only slightly overstates the case when he writes that the Sermon on the Mount in Matt 5–7 is "unintelligible" if it is "isolated from its context within Matthew's Gospel."[3] Hauerwas contends that when the Sermon is "isolated," it becomes a "law" or an "ethic." And of course many

---

2. Typically, the discourses begin with some statement indicating that Jesus began to speak or teach (5:2; 10:5; 13:3; 18:2; 24:3–4) and end with the note that Jesus "had finished" the parables or instructing his disciples (8:1; 11:1; 13:53; 19:1; 26:1).

3. Stanley Hauerwas, *Matthew*, Brazos Theological Commentary on the Bible (Grand Rapids: Brazos, 2006), 102.

interpreters have wrestled with the Sermon on precisely those grounds: What sort of law is this, what kind of ethic?[4]

Even if it is somewhat exaggerated to say that the Sermon is "unintelligible" unless it is read as part of a narrative, reading it as part of a narrative does shape how it is understood. Narratives are often spoken of as having two levels, the "story level" and the "discourse" (or "rhetorical") level.[5] The story level consists of the basic features that distinguish a narrative from other forms of literature, such as the events, setting, and characters; the discourse level of the narrative refers to how the story is told and what it intends to do or bring about. Here, features such as sequence, plot, point of view, and structural patterns are important.

A Gospel is a narrative, an interpreted account of who Jesus was, and of the kinds of things that he said and did, what kind of people responded to him in what ways, how his public ministry led ultimately to his death, and what happened next. Matthew wants to tell that story in order to fulfill the commission given at the end of the Gospel itself: to make disciples of all people. As has often been said, the Gospels were intended to make saints, not historians. In other words, at the level of its discourse, Matthew intends to form faithful disciples of Jesus, the Messiah, the main character of this narrative account. How it does that is not always straightforward, because narratives seldom carry their own interpretive guidelines with them. For example, narratives seldom explain which characters or which of their actions are exemplary or laudatory or to be imitated, if at all. So how the narrative of Matthew works to form its readers is left in large measure to their own discernment. Surely the words of Jesus—his instruction—play a large role in forming disciples. But they do so in the context of a narrative of Jesus' life, including his deeds, death, and resurrection. The whole of this narrative shapes the life of Jesus' followers.

---

4. Talbert, *Reading the Sermon on the Mount*, and McKnight, *Sermon on the Mount*, both discuss the Sermon with respect to the various types of ethics, such as consequentialist, deontological, virtue, and so on.

5. Seymour Chatman, *Story and Discourse: Narrative Structure in Fiction and Film* (Ithaca: Cornell University Press, 1978), spoke of "story" and "discourse"; David M. Rhoads and Donald Michie, *Mark as Story: An Introduction to the Narrative of a Gospel*, 3rd ed. (Minneapolis: Fortress, 2012), refer to the levels of "story" and "rhetoric." See also Jeannine K. Brown, *The Gospels as Stories: A Narrative Approach to Matthew, Mark, Luke, and John* (Grand Rapids: Baker Academic, 2020), 11–19.

Matthew's Gospel as Narrative

Matthew's narrative has a beginning, a middle, and an end. Its central character, Jesus, is introduced by means of his genealogy, birth, and baptism, which together lead to the episode of his temptations in the wilderness. When these are ended, we read, "From that time on, Jesus began to proclaim, 'Repent, for the kingdom of heaven has come near'" (4:17). John the Baptist had preached the same message, but following Jesus' baptism and temptation, Jesus began to announce the approaching kingdom. Matthew then portrays Jesus instructing the crowds, telling parables, performing miracles and exorcisms—and creating significant conflict. As a result of all this and more, Peter confesses that Jesus is the Messiah, the Son of the living God. And then we read, "From that time on, Jesus began to show his disciples that he must go to Jerusalem and undergo great suffering at the hands of the elders and chief priests and scribes, and be killed, and on the third day be raised" (16:21).

This chronological note—"from that time on"—marks two significant shifts in the narrative. From the time of his baptism and temptation, Jesus proclaimed the kingdom; from the time of Peter's confession, Jesus joins that proclamation with announcements regarding his death. Given the material that is yet to come in Matthew, especially Jesus' triumphal entry into Jerusalem as king (21:5), it is clear that the kingdom proclamation has not ceased or been replaced: but it is now decisively shaped so as to aim toward and include the events of Jesus' crucifixion and death.

Matthew's Gospel is thus a narrative of conflict. From the time of his birth, Jesus' life is threatened by ruling powers. Herod the Great seeks to destroy Jesus, because this "king of the Jews" can brook no opposition to his rule. The forerunner of Jesus, John the Baptist, announces that the kingdom of heaven has come near and warns of impending judgment: here is God's power at work to judge, to cut down, to burn up all that stands against God's straight paths. Jesus aligns himself with John's message of the kingdom and is anointed—empowered—by God's Spirit, as the Son of God. Following a period in the wilderness, Jesus proclaims the nearness of the kingdom of heaven, an announcement not likely to put King Herod's successor at ease!

At the outset of his public work, Jesus called his first disciples, "went up the mountain," sat down, and began to teach (5:1–2). Given the context of Jesus' initial instructions one is primed for a prophetic denunciation, like John's, against the religious leaders, or against the unjust acts of

Herod the Great and his sons and heirs. Jesus' opening words, about the blessings to be expected by the meek, poor in spirit, and merciful, hardly seem designed to challenge the tyrannical powers at work in the world or to explain the conflict that marks the narrative. But as has already been suggested, the conflict in Matthew is explained not only by what Jesus says and does, but by who he is.

Jesus the Preacher

As noted, the "Sermon on the Mount" is introduced by the statement that "Jesus went up on the mountain," sat down, and began to teach.[6] Given the statement that "Jesus went up on the mountain," and that the law and its interpretation play an important role in the Sermon, many interpreters have understood Matthew to have drawn a comparison between Jesus and Moses. Moses was, of course, known as a lawgiver, but in Jewish tradition he also became known as a prophet and, in that role, as a type of Messiah.[7] Moses, no stranger to conflict, was also the one who, standing against pharaoh, ruler of Egypt, led the Israelites out of captivity en route to the promised land. Does Matthew, then, portray Jesus as a "new Moses," challenging the ruling powers, calling his people together and leading them forward, and teaching the law, or perhaps giving a new law?

While the comparison to Moses may only be implicit, by this point in the narrative, Jesus has been introduced explicitly with a variety of designations, which together explain who he is. Jesus' birth is the sign of Immanuel, that "God is with us" (1:23); later, the risen Jesus promises that he will be with his people until "the close of the age" (28:20). According to the genealogy that opens the Gospel, Jesus is the son of David, the son of Abraham. Abraham is the father of Israel; David, its paradigmatic king. Having introduced Jesus as the son of Abraham, the genealogy traces the

---

6. The statement that someone "went up on the mountain" occurs eighteen times in the Pentateuch (LXX), with most of these referring to Moses. After receiving the Torah, Moses "went down" from the mountain (Exod 34:29), even as Jesus went down from the mountain after finishing his Sermon. For an examination of the parallels in detail, see Dale C. Allison, *The New Moses: A Matthean Typology* (Eugene, OR: Wipf & Stock, 2013). Allison contends that "Jesus is the Moses-like Messiah who proclaims the eschatological will of God on a mountain typologically equated with Sinai" (185).

7. The prophecy of Deut 18:15–18, that God would raise up another "prophet like Moses," was understood to refer to a future coming figure by, among others, Samaritans; see John 4:25–26 for the expectation of a prophetic Messiah.

story of the rise and fall of Israel's kingdom, of its glory under David and its loss to Babylon, ending with the birth of Jesus the Messiah, the son of David.[8] All of these designations bode well for Israel, the people of God. One might well ask: How will this Messiah, the son of Abraham and David, tell the story of Israel, the story of the people of God?

That Jesus is designated the son of Abraham, who is the "father" of Israel, alerts us to references in the Gospel to the people of Israel. From Bethlehem comes a ruler who "is to shepherd my people Israel" (2:6). Later, Jesus will be portrayed as looking for a response to his proclamation of the kingdom among the lost sheep of the people of Israel (8:10; 9:33; 10:6; 15:24). Having appointed twelve as the foundation of the messianic people he is calling together, Jesus promises that the Twelve will "sit on twelve thrones, judging the twelve tribes of Israel" (19:28). Indeed, as the king of Israel (27:42), Jesus' work is to gather together God's people, all the children of Abraham.

As the king of Israel, Jesus is the son of David. The sick and needy appeal to the son of David for healing for themselves and others (9:27; 15:22; 20:30). People sing praise to Jesus as the son of David, who comes in the name of the Lord (21:9, 15). When Jesus himself poses the question "Whose son is the Messiah?," the answer seems obvious: "The son of David" (22:42). Would not this Messiah, the heir of the kingdom overthrown by Babylon, now overthrow the "Babylon" of his time?

Three key terms in Matthew's narrative thus far—kingdom, Israel, and Messiah—belong together and account for the raised hopes of the triumphal entry. In too many Hollywood movies and contemporary reading of the Gospels, the most pressing question on the hearts and minds of first-century Jews must surely have been "When will the Messiah come?" But while the literature from this period does refer, now and again, to various messianic expectations, its most pressing questions are found elsewhere. More specifically, the literature demonstrates the regular concern to deal with the question "What does it mean to be the people of God?" The answers might vary: but they would all focus on obedience to and worship of the one God as shown forth in adherence to the law. To worship one God and to keep his law are at the heart of what it means to

---

8. Matthew's genealogy traces Jesus' heritage through the royal line and David's son Solomon. The genealogy itself is divided into three sets of fourteen generations each: these three "sets" run from Abraham to David; from David the king to the demise of the kingship with the "deportation to Babylon" (1:11); and then "after the deportation to Babylon" to Jesus, "who is called the Messiah."

be God's people. But *how* this law was to be understood and lived out was the source of significant disagreements: these disagreements are evident in the literature of the Dead Sea Scrolls; they are documented in early rabbinic texts, such as the Mishnah; and they appear in the New Testament, including the Gospels. How ought one to observe the Sabbath? What obligations does one have to the poor? What law governs marriage and divorce? Which interpretation, and which teacher of the law, should we follow? These are not first questions about the legitimacy of the law, or whether to keep it, but questions about how to live out the commandments of God and so how to be God's people.

The New Testament is replete with the concern for what it means to be the people of God, whether that question focuses on the place of the gentiles, the keeping of the law, or the patterns that are to shape the behavior of God's people. While Matthew is a narrative about the son of Abraham, the son of David, the Son of God, the Messiah of Israel, its interest in Jesus' identity is always linked with the question of the identity and practices of God's people. So, what does it mean to be the people of God, according to Matthew? What kind of community does Jesus in Matthew want to create?

The answer to this question may seem to be most apparent in the teaching material of the Gospel although, as we shall see, the answer is not limited to the didactic material. But both in the words and deeds of Jesus, the Gospel of Matthew describes and calls for a community that learns how to live in the kingdom from Jesus, the son of David, the Messiah; the people learn what it means to be Israel, from the true Israelite, the son of Abraham; they learn how to live out the law, received by Moses, from the one who taught what lay at its heart; and they learn what it means as the children of the ever-present God to trust in God, following the Son of God. *Who* Jesus is therefore indicates *what* his concerns are going to be, and how the Sermon fits with and flows from his identity. We turn then to a closer look at the words of Jesus in his first major "discourse" to his people.

The Sermon That Jesus Preaches

The Sermon is the first of five discourses that describe what it means to be the people of God gathered by Jesus.[9] It follows on Jesus' call for repentance

---

9. The Sermon on the Mount is a compilation of the words of Jesus, and most likely owes its present framing, structure, and the selection of content to the author of Matthew. John Calvin, *A Harmony of the Gospels: Matthew, Mark and Luke*, trans. A. W.

in light of the coming kingdom and lays out what that life of repentance looks like. The theme of the Sermon on the Mount is what it means to live before God, to trust in God with all one's heart, soul, and mind: and to do so now in the time of the approaching kingdom announced by Jesus, the messianic interpreter of God's will and purposes. The Beatitudes, which promise blessing to those who live in accord with God's kingly rule, open the Sermon, introducing the postures and practices that are spelled out in what follows. The Sermon then moves from Jesus' teaching regarding the shape and demand of the righteousness that mirrors God's perfection, into various instructions on piety, praying and the Lord's Prayer, and then back again to further instruction regarding doing the will of the Father. Emphasizing the seriousness of what is at stake, the Sermon ends with an echo of the "two ways" teaching found in Scripture, Judaism, and early Christianity (7:13–15) that envisions two paths of life: that of the wise and of the foolish; of the righteous and the wicked; the way of life and the way of death. Jesus pictures the wise and the foolish as those who, respectively, hear or ignore his words (7:24–27). One builds on the rock; the other on the sand. One withstands the onslaughts of life; the other collapses. One enters the narrow gate, leading to life; the other, the wide gate, leading to the broad path of destruction.

But to go back to the beginning, the Sermon begins with the "Beatitudes," those statements pronouncing blessings on people who are living in particular ways. This is how the people whom Jesus wishes to gather together are to live. Much ink has been spilled over the question whether the Beatitudes are "descriptive," depicting the kinds of people and practices who elicit or merit God's blessing upon them, or whether they are "prescriptive," calling for these kinds of behaviors. In her recent work, Rebecca Eklund has shown that in the history of reception, this distinction cannot be made in the abstract, apart from a specific social context and that, indeed, sometimes it cannot and need not be made at all.[10] Jesus, who

---

Morrison; ed. David W. Torrance and Thomas F. Torrance (Grand Rapids: Eerdmans, 1972), calls the Sermon "a short summary of the teaching of Christ, gathered from many and various discourses, of which this was the first, where he spoke with his disciples on the true blessedness" (1:168). Scot McKnight notes that the Sermon consists of "clearly discernible topics about discipleship that move one to another" (*Sermon on the Mount*, 25). For further discussion, see Dale C. Allison, "The Structure of the Sermon on the Mount," *Journal of Biblical Literature* 106 (1987) 431–32.

10. Rebekah Eklund, *The Beatitudes Through the Ages* (Grand Rapids: Eerdmans, 2021).

proclaims these blessings, assumes that there are people who *are* living as the Beatitudes describe and that they *ought* to be living as the Beatitudes describe. The Sermon itself will spell out what it means to be meek, poor in spirit, peacemakers, pure in heart, and so on. You're on the right road, Jesus says, if you live like that: you will have found that narrow way.

The Sermon is a call to a wholehearted, single-minded allegiance to the one God of Israel. Jesus calls his disciples to seek first the kingdom of God: that is, to live so that God's kingly rule and purposes shape all of life (6:33). To seek first the kingdom is to serve God wholeheartedly. "No one," Jesus warns, "can serve two masters" (6:24). The master who merits such single-minded devotion is known, here and throughout Matthew, as a faithful father. Jesus instructs his disciples to pray to God, together, as "our Father," trusting in God's provision for their daily needs (6:9–13). This father provides shelter, protection, and food for all his creation—lilies, birds, human beings (6:25–34). This father gives good gifts to his children who ask for what they need (7:7–11). After all, God watches over the sparrow, and God's children are of more value than they (10:29–31). This father can be trusted, even when the rewards or blessings for faithfulness and trust are not publicly visible and justice is not easily discernible, if at all: giving alms, fasting, and praying are done in secret, out of public view, but those who do these things can be assured that their father hears and acknowledges in secret (6:1–6). God sees. Jesus' disciples are to love their enemies in imitation of the impartiality and generosity of their father who sends the blessings of rain on the righteous and unrighteous alike. When God's generous goodness flows into one's life and heart, it will and must flow out again to others. This is the "perfection" of God one is to imitate and practice. The Sermon on the Mount is resolutely theocentric, describing and calling for the purity of heart that wills one thing: allegiance to one God.

One of the key aspects not only of the Sermon itself, but of the entire Gospel of Matthew as well, is the presentation of Jesus as the definitive interpreter of the law: the law is to be kept, but it is to be kept as interpreted by Jesus (5:17–48; 7:12). Jesus calls his disciples to a righteousness "that exceeds that of the scribes and Pharisees." This righteousness is pictured in the Beatitudes and spelled out in the Sermon; it is epitomized in Jesus' "double love command." When asked about the greatest commandment in the law, Jesus replies: "'You shall love the Lord your God with all your heart, and with all your soul, and with all your mind.' This is the greatest and first commandment. And a second is like it: 'You shall love your neighbor as yourself.' *On these two commandments hang all the law and the prophets"* (Matt 22:34-40). Love of God and love of neighbor are the core of the law: everything else derives from them. Or, in the terms Jesus uses, found also in rabbinic descriptions of the commandments, some matters of the law are weightier than others: there are commands that are at the heart of the law, and all the rest depend or "hang" on them.[11]

So when Jesus excoriates the Pharisees, he states, "You tithe mint, and dill and cumin, but you have neglected the weightier matters of the law, justice, and mercy and faith; these you ought to have done without neglecting the others" (23:23). The whole law holds together: but it is bound together by the weightier matters of justice, mercy, and faith. Thus in Matthew Jesus twice quotes God's words from Hosea, "I desire mercy, and not sacrifice," to justify his actions of eating with sinners and giving grain to his hungry disciples on the Sabbath (9:13; 12:7; cf. 7:21-27; 18:33; 20:15). Love and mercy guide interpretation of the law, because they are the heart of God's will. Jesus' interpretation of the heart of the law does not set love over against law, but instead insists that the heart of God's law is to be found in mercy, in love of the other.

All of this can be found in the Scriptures of Israel. The prophets had interpreted the heart of the law, of God's will, in terms of mercy, justice, and kindness (Isa 58:6-7; Jer 7:3-4; Hos 6:6; Amos 5:21-24), warning of the consequences of injustice and neglect of the poor. Thus when asked to weigh in on a dispute or issue of biblical interpretation, Jesus replies with the challenge "Have you not read . . . ?" or "Have you never read . . . ?" (12:3, 5; 19:4; 21:16, 42; 22:31). It's all there in Scripture. Have you not read what David did on the Sabbath when he and his men were hungry? Have you never read that the stone that the builders rejected has become the head of the corner? Jesus challenges his hearers to read the Scriptures—but to read them as he interprets them. The Scriptures are intended to teach, but also to stir people from complacency. And so the words of Jesus, like the words of the prophets before him, judge and divide.

It is sometimes suggested that what distinguished Jesus' teaching in the Sermon on the Mount was his stress on interiority: no longer is it enough to obey the commandment not to murder—one must not be angry (5:21-22); no longer is it enough not to commit adultery—one must

---

11. According to the Talmud, Hillel is said to have summarized the whole Torah in one law, "Whatever is hateful to you, do not do to your neighbor; this is the whole Torah, everything else is explanation" (b. Sabb 31a). Similarly, Aqiba is quoted as teaching, "This is the great principle of the Torah: Love your neighbor as yourself" (Ber. Rabbah 24:7).

not look at a woman with "lust in his heart" (5:27–28). As Jesus says, "In the same way, every good tree bears good fruit, but the bad tree bears bad fruit. A good tree cannot bear bad fruit, nor can a bad tree bear good fruit. Every tree that does not bear good fruit is cut down and thrown into the fire. Thus you will know them by their fruits" (7:17). Jesus repeats the point later: "Either make the tree good, and its fruit good; or make the tree bad, and its fruit bad; for the tree is known by its fruit" (12:33). If one wants good fruit, one must change the tree. What Jesus calls for requires an inner transformation of the "heart" that issues in specific conduct, spelled out in the Sermon in terms of doing good to one's neighbor (7:12). That is why Jesus can say, "Not everyone who says to me, 'Lord, Lord,' will enter the kingdom of heaven, but only the one who does the will of my Father in heaven" (7:21). Doing the will of the Father is evidence of the transformation that Jesus calls for.

But this call, too, is known in the Scriptures of Israel. The psalmist spoke of his delight to do God's will, because the law was "within my heart" (40:8). And yet, acknowledging that God desires "truth in the inward being," the psalmist petitions God to teach him wisdom in his "secret heart," and to create a "clean heart" and "new and right spirit within" him (51:10). The prophet Jeremiah foresees a day when the law of God will be written on hearts of flesh, not stone (31:33; cf. Ezek 18:30–32; 36:26–27). Human beings do not naturally live in alignment with the will and purposes of God; the psalmist and prophets proclaimed that God must create and renew the heart precisely so that one may live in allegiance to God's ways. So, too, Jesus warned, "Out of the heart come evil intentions, murder, adultery, fornication, theft, false witness, slander" (Matt 15:19). A bad tree produces bad fruit. Not everyone does the will of his Father. The righteousness that exceeds that of the scribes and Pharisees, that represents a life that is aligned with God's purposes, requires an inner transformation that issues in specific conduct.

The Sermon calls for a wholehearted allegiance to the one God, the Father; such allegiance manifests itself in generosity, kindness, and mercy to others. Those who have received mercy ought to demonstrate that mercy. Those who have received forgiveness bestow the same forgiveness on others: Jesus teaches his disciples to pray, "Forgive us our debts, as we forgive our debtors." So another of Jesus' five discourses in Matthew—the one most clearly demonstrating Matthew's "ecclesiastical bent"—spells out how Jesus' *ekklesia* is to live together: showing forbearance, forgiveness, and seeking out the sheep who has gone astray (18:15–22). The point is driven home by the parable of the unmerciful servant: having been forgiven an enormous debt by his master, the unmerciful servant refuses to forgive a fellow servant a much smaller debt. The parable graphically depicts the issue: the servant who has just received mercy is not simply to *feel* grateful; he is to do as has been done to him. Not only do human beings find it hard to show mercy, they often begrudge the mercy bestowed on others, as the parable of the laborers in the vineyard makes clear. Having worked unequal lengths of time during the day, all the workers receive the same wages, and those who worked the longest and received the same as all the others grumbled about their treatment. "Why do you grumble?" the landowner asks. "Do you begrudge my generosity?" (20:1–15).

We have noted that, in the Sermon, Jesus calls people to wholehearted trust in God, while simultaneously summarizing the "law and the prophets" in terms of how we should treat others: "In everything do to others as you would have them do to you" (7:12). Love of God and love for others belong together; those who have received mercy are to show mercy. Thus we note that while, in the Sermon on the Mount, Jesus asks his disciples to "consider the lilies of the field" and to trust in their Father's generous provision for food, clothing, and shelter, he later tells a parable in which the sheep and the goats are separated based on whether they had provided the necessities of life—food, clothing, shelter—to others. He does not identify the sheep as those who were interiorly disposed toward God and the goats as those who were not. The sheep are those who had treated the "least of these" with the kind of generosity and mercy shown to them.

In Matthew, Jesus is calling together a people whose allegiances are to God and God's kingdom—and that necessarily entails a commitment to those in that kingdom, forgiving them, providing for them, showing them mercy. This conduct is summarized in the Beatitudes, described in the Sermon, and echoed throughout Jesus' teaching in Matthew. This conduct flows from meekness, purity of heart, gentleness of spirit, peacemaking, and the hunger for righteousness, and issues in deeds that embody the mercy and righteousness of God. The Sermon describes a life that manifests the repentance appropriate to the coming kingdom.

The Sermon That Jesus Embodies

Thus far we have focused on what Jesus teaches in the Sermon and throughout Matthew about the way of life to which he calls his disciples. If we were to end our discussion here, we could then raise a host of questions about what exactly Jesus instructs people to do, what sort of ethic this might be, and whether it is realistic. Here it is worth calling to mind again Hauerwas's comment that the Sermon becomes "unintelligible" if isolated from its narrative context. He goes on to say that the Sermon becomes an ethic, or a law, when what is taught is abstracted from the teacher. "When the sermon is isolated from the one alone who is the exemplification of righteousness, it seems natural to ask if all Jesus's teachings must be followed literally. Does Jesus really think it possible for us to live without lust? How would we be able to run the world if we do not resist evildoers? Once such questions are allowed to determine how the sermon is read, strategies are developed to help us avoid thinking that it applies to our lives."[12]

Hauerwas aptly underscores the importance of reading Matthew as a narrative and reading the Sermon within that narrative. Only in this way are preacher and sermon brought together. Jesus is not just a sage dispensing wisdom to his disciples, a new Moses teaching the heart of the law. He is the faithful Israelite who lives out what he teaches; the King of Israel gathering a people who will live in the way he prescribes. He does not ask anything of his disciples which he has not himself already put into practice or which he will not put into practice. What it means to learn discipleship from Jesus is not only to learn what he instructed others to do, but to live as he lived, trusting in God with heart, soul, and mind. Jesus' own trust in God is epitomized in the words with which he is taunted as he hangs, dying on the cross: "He saved others; he cannot save himself. He is the King of Israel; let him come down from the cross now, and we will believe in him. *He trusts in God*; let God deliver him now, if he wants to; for he said, 'I am God's Son'" (Matt 27:42–43). Matthew's narrative depicts this son of Abraham, the son of David, the Son of God, from beginning to end, "trusting God." The narrative shows Jesus living out the words of this "sermon" that calls for humble trust in and single-minded allegiance to God, even when he is simultaneously moved to cry out, "My God, my God; why have you forsaken me?" (Matt 27:46).

---

12. Hauerwas, *Matthew*, 101–4. He further argues that such an approach wrongly separates the person and work of Christ.

The Sermon on the Mount

Matthew's narrative will show that Jesus' trust in God was vindicated, leading as it does to his resurrection and to God's granting to him "all authority in heaven and on earth": but Jesus dies *trusting* in God's vindication. While the Sermon on the Mount calls for radical trust in God, the narrative shows what this trust looks like. Jesus' life, as Matthew depicts it throughout his narrative, from the first days when Herod's bloody edict threatens it, to the cross when he gives it up, makes plain what such trust might cost. The narrative of Matthew shows that the Sermon's instructions and admonitions are to be lived out in following Jesus as his disciple, because Jesus himself puts them into practice. We can look briefly at how this works out in the Gospel.

Following his baptism, Jesus withdraws to the wilderness, to be tempted by the devil (4:1). The narrative echoes that of Israel in the wilderness in Deuteronomy (chs. 6–8). Unlike the Israelites, Jesus, the son of Abraham, the true Israelite, resists all the temptations to turn away from God or to grumble against God's provision. Each time, Jesus does so by citing a Scripture that calls for trusting reliance on and devotion to God alone. Even though he is hungry, Jesus will not use the power of the Spirit given to him as the Son of God at his baptism to turn stones to bread. "One does not live by bread alone," he notes, "but by every word that proceeds from the mouth of God" (Deut 8:3). In the context of Deuteronomy, Moses reminds his people that God fed and clothed them for forty years in their wanderings. So, too, Jesus calls on his disciples to trust in God for the provision of food, clothing, and shelter. He lived in such trust, explaining that while foxes have holes and birds have nests, he himself had no fixed home. He sent his disciples out on a mission to announce the approaching kingdom, commanding them to take nothing, but to rely on others for provisions and hospitality. Jesus himself fed the hungry multitudes (14:13–21; 15:33–37) and envisioned a kingdom that welcomed those who had generously provided for others (25:31–46).

In the third temptation, the devil offered Jesus all the "kingdoms of the world" if Jesus would worship him. Apparently the gratification would be immediate, demonstrable, powerful: not like the wheat growing among the weeds or the partial crop the sower gets for his work. But Jesus does what he commands his followers to do: he seeks first, and above all, God's kingdom, offering complete obedience to God. Everything here depends on Jesus' understanding of the kingdom, what it entails, what it brings, and what it does not entail or bring. Jesus continued to announce God's kingdom, even riding into Jerusalem on a donkey and receiving the royal welcome due a king, although it was surely his claims to kingship and the imminent kingdom that brought Rome's wrath down upon him. The Gospel shows that Jesus knew what commitment to God and the messianic vocation given to him would cost: and yet he would not turn aside from it, when friend or foe offered another way.

In the second temptation, the devil suggested that Jesus put God to the test, to see if God would honor his promises. According to Ps 91, "'[God] will command his angels concerning you,' and 'On their hands they will bear you up, so that you will not dash your foot against a stone'" (Matt 4:6). Surely, the devil says, God will want you to be able to trust him: why not do a reality check now to see if he is trustworthy? But Jesus refuses: "You shall not test the Lord your God" (Deut 6:16). This is the whole point of the temptations: to get Jesus to turn from trusting God and to take matters into his own hands; to get Jesus to turn from following God's straight paths, to paths of his own making. This temptation arises again when, following Peter's confession of him as "the Messiah, the Son of the living God," Jesus introduces the disciples to the fact that he will suffer and be crucified. Peter is horrified, protesting that this will never happen to Jesus. Jesus' reply, "Get behind me, Satan! You are a stumbling block to me; for you are setting your mind not on divine things but on human things" (16:23) puts us right back into the narrative of the temptations and into the heart of the Sermon: no one can serve two masters; seek first the kingdom of God; your will be done.

"Your will be done." It is one of the petitions of the Lord's Prayer that Jesus teaches, lodged in the center of the Sermon. It glosses the petition "your kingdom come."[13] For God's kingdom to come will mean that God's will is being done. To pray "your will be done" means that those praying it desire to follow God's will. It is the one who "does the will of my Father in heaven" who enters the kingdom (7:21). Whoever "does the will of my Father in heaven" belongs to Jesus' family (12:50).[14] Two sons were sent to work in the vineyard, but it is the one who actually went who "did the

---

13. For a discussion of the links between the Lord's Prayer and Matthew, see Marianne Meye Thompson, "Lex Orandi, Lex Vivendi: A Theological Interpretation of Discipleship in the Gospel of Matthew," in *Ears That Hear: Explorations in Theological Interpretation of the Bible*, ed. Joel Green and Tim Meadowcroft (Sheffield: Phoenix, 2013), 114–29.

14. The phrases "the will of my father" and "the will of your father" are unique to Matthew (7:21; 12:50; 18:14; 21:31; 26:42); the descriptive phrase "the one who does the will of my father" is essentially a description of a disciple of Jesus.

will of his Father" (21:31). Your will be done is a prayer with two prongs: God must act to accomplish his will; but Jesus' disciples are also to live in accord with God's will. That will is sometimes mysterious, and hidden, revealed not to the wise but to infants, as Jesus acknowledges later (11:25–26), and it may perhaps seem never more mysterious than when Jesus prays "your will be done" in Gethsemane. Suddenly, Jesus' words "not everyone who says to me, 'Lord, Lord!' will enter the kingdom of heaven, but only those who do the will of my Father in heaven" (7:21) take on a new cast. "Lord, Lord" or "Your will be done" are easy to say: but the narrative of Matthew shows that God's will does cost Jesus everything. No wonder Jesus counsels his disciples, "Pray that you enter not into temptation" (26:41). It is all too easy to turn to the easy road and the wide gate (7:13). That Jesus teaches his disciples to pray "your will be done" and prays it himself in his hour of greatest distress shows, again, Jesus living in the reliance on God for which he had called.

Jesus also taught his disciples to pray "forgive us our sins." Throughout the narrative, we see Jesus forgiving sins, as in the healing of the paralytic (9:2–5), and eating together with "many tax collectors and sinners" (9:10–13; 11:19). Such practices were not good for Jesus' reputation: he was called a glutton, a drunkard, a friend of sinners. One notes the irony, then, when Jesus rouses his sleeping disciples in the Gethsemane with the words "the Son of Man is betrayed into the hands of sinners" (26:45). Jesus' ministry, his life and death, are directed toward those who have need of a physician, to the sick: to sinners. And "sinners" includes those who are responsible for his crucifixion. As Jesus says at the Last Supper to his disciples, according to Matthew, "This is my blood of the covenant, which is poured out for many for the forgiveness of sins" (26:28).

Jesus will give everything to accomplish this mission. He had manifested the kingdom through exorcism and healing, even though his deeds, the occasions on which he did them, and his scriptural justifications for them risked the backlash of the authorities and no doubt the rejection of the people. Jesus' understanding of the kingdom and his role in it were not intended to win friends and influence people. He called his people to live together in a way that made forgiveness, mercy, humility, and generosity the prevailing norms. Jesus' way was not one of the popular options for being the people of God. When opposition led eventually to his arrest, Jesus refused to take up the sword to defend himself (26:51), even as he had admonished his hearers not to resist an evildoer but to "turn the other cheek" (5:39). Jesus' refusal to "resist" the evildoer who came to arrest him, his willingness to "turn the other cheek," shows the lengths to which he will go for the sake of the kingdom of God and the will of his Father. He thus calls would-be disciples to "take up their cross" and follow him in the way of giving oneself up even to death (10:38; 16:24–25). Jesus' blood of the covenant, poured out for the forgiveness of sins, requires that the members of the covenant live in a way commensurate with his own life, devoted to God and God's kingdom.

A Closing Word

There is no doubt that Matthew presents Jesus as a teacher; in fact, as an able teacher. When Jesus asks the disciples, following his explanation of the parables, whether they have "understood all this," they answer, "Yes" (13:51). We are not meant to smirk. And yet Jesus' words do not meet with universal acclamation: instead, they divide those who hear them from those who do not; those who find the "narrow gate" and those who do not. These words are meant to form a people and, as so often in Scripture, not all the people of God welcome the words of their prophets. Jesus' first discourse, the Sermon on the Mount, lays out the shape of life to which he calls the people of Israel. This is how they are to live together; this is what they are to be and to do.

But the Sermon must not be turned into a checklist of right conduct. As is often pointed out, the sheep in the parable of judgment at the end of Matthew had not done the right thing out of mercenary calculation: they were simply living out the way of the kingdom. In the end, all of Jesus' words and teaching belong within the framework of the Gospel narrative, in which Jesus not only instructs the multitudes but calls disciples to follow him. To follow him means to hear and do what he says; but it also means to live as he lived, to risk what he risked: to trust as he trusted.

2

The Sermon on the Mount as Law and Gospel

Piotr J. Małysz

TO SPEAK OF THE Sermon on the Mount as both law and gospel requires some preliminary ground clearing. It calls for awareness—hermeneutical as well as theological—of what exactly it is we are trying to accomplish. First of all, we should be aware of the danger of imposing on the Sermon an alien framework, a straitjacket, or at least all-too-easy a mold that will prevent us from hearing the Sermon in all its complexity. It could be said, of course, that law and gospel are merely a matter of preaching, of interpreting and applying a text to our audience. But if that is the case, it is even more imperative that we first hear the text and wrestle with its own unruliness before rather confidently—confidently because prematurely—holding it hostage to whatever we consider pastorally relevant.

Still, even when we do make time for the text and allow it its own voice, it is not yet obvious how exactly we should make room for it. To state the obvious, the Sermon on the Mount belongs to Matthew's Gospel; and it, moreover, has its specific location within it. Matthew's Gospel is a literary whole and, as Ulrich Luz has argued, also a catechetical whole.[1] It was originally written to be heard in its entirety in one sitting, though certainly not just once but multiple times. The Gospel has its integrity and

---

1. Ulrich Luz, "Matthew the Evangelist: A Jewish Christian at the Crossroads," in *Studies in Matthew*, trans. Rosemary Selle (Grand Rapids: Eerdmans, 2005), 3–17.

its "Aha!" moments. Within the Gospel, the Sermon on the Mount is the first of five teaching discourses that come from Jesus' lips. And it belongs, more broadly, to the beginning of Jesus' ministry that will eventually lead him to the cross and then beyond death to yet another—though perhaps the very same—mountain in Galilee. There he will yet again address his (now eleven) disciples, leaving them with an abiding promise, "And remember, I am with you always, to the end of the age" (Matt 28:20). When we take all this into account, how we allow the text to present itself to us will, then, in no small measure determine how much we can realistically, responsibly, and respectfully ask of it.

With these two caveats—recognition that our own questions may be just that: our own questions; as well as awareness that texts speak out of broader narrative locations, both textual and in a complex way also historical—we may now undertake a very preliminary foray into Jesus' Sermon on the Mount as presented to us by the evangelist Matthew.

Law and Gospel in the Sermon

The lens of law and gospel does seem to be a handy device allowing us to make sense of the text before us. We can not only categorize the text but also establish a path through it. The text comes into focus and becomes navigable. We can, as it were, see through it. The framework itself is simple, or so it appears. We turn briefly to Martin Luther to supply the definitions. "At its briefest," writes Luther, "the gospel is a discourse about Christ, that he is the Son of God and became man for us, that he died and was raised, that he has been established as a Lord over all things."[2] Luther's echo of the creedal "for us and for our salvation" is of fundamental importance here. The gospel has to do with God's action. This action has taken place in Christ, outside and irrespective of our own doing. But it is, nonetheless, meant for us. As such, it can, thus, come to us only purely gratuitously, as a gift. "The Gospel teaches that Christ was born for our sake and that he did everything and suffered all things for our sake," Luther explains in a Christmas Eve sermon.[3] Faced with the gospel, we can

---

2. Martin Luther, "A Brief Instruction on What to Look for and Expect in the Gospels," *Luther's Works*, American ed., 82 vols. (St. Louis and Philadelphia: Concordia and Fortress, 1955–) [hereafter cited as *LW*], 35:118.

3. Luther's sermon on the gospel for Christmas Eve (Luke 2), *LW* 52:14. The sermon appeared, together with "A Brief Instruction," in the 1522 *Weihnachtspostille*.

be only recipients—those who take God's action for what it is, his action *for us*. In relation to the gospel, we can be only believers. And insofar as we take God's action-in-Christ to be for us, it acquires in our lives the status of a fundamental and all-embracing promise.

Luther is far from denying, of course, that Jesus also had something to say to people's own actions and their conduct. Neither does Luther deny that Jesus can also serve as an example for us to imitate with our own actions (though, with Jesus being the Son of God, the scope of our imitation of him is rather limited[4]). "Now when Christ has thus [through faith in the gospel] become your own, and when you through him have become cleansed in such faith, then you have received your inheritance and the chief goods, without any merit of your own, as you see, but solely because of God's love who gives to you as your own his Son's possessions and works. Now there follows the example of good works, that you also do to your neighbor as you see that Christ has done for you."[5] Still, given that Christ can be understood as both gift and example, Luther is very much concerned that the integrity of the Gospel should in no way be compromised. He warns: "Be sure . . . that you do not make Christ into a Moses, as if Christ did nothing more than teach and provide examples as the other saints do, as if the gospel were simply a textbook of teachings or laws."[6] All of this can be summed up rather handily: "The law says, 'do this,' and it is never done. Grace [which Luther understands as God's favor manifested in God's actions for us] says, 'believe in this,' and everything is already done."[7] Or, in an even broader definition that bypasses the explicitly imperative form of the law, "Whatever is not grace is Law, whether it be the Civil Law, the Ceremonial Law, or the Decalog."[8]

When we bring this lens to the Sermon on the Mount, on the face of it it might seem that the Sermon is all law, its import being fundamentally ethical. To put it bluntly, there seems to be no gospel in it. This appears to be actually confirmed by several well-worn statements of Jesus, such as "I have not come to abolish [the law and the prophets] but to fulfill. For truly I tell you, until heaven and earth pass away, not one letter, not one stroke of a letter, will pass from the law until all is accomplished" (5:17–18). To be sure,

---

4. "Against the Heavenly Prophets," *LW* 40:131–32.
5. "Sermon on the Gospel for Christmas Eve," *LW* 52:16.
6. "A Brief Instruction," *LW* 35:119.
7. "Heidelberg Disputation," *LW* 31:56.
8. "Lectures on Galatians," *LW* 26:122.

it is possible to argue that underlying the term *nomos* in Matthew's Greek is the Hebrew *torah*, with all its variegated teachings, and that this broader scope of *nomos* is reinforced by Jesus' pairing the law up with the prophets, thus indicating the entire theological-textual lore of Israel. But this reading appears immediately undercut by Jesus' own elaboration, which after the broad gesture rapidly moves in the direction of law much more narrowly understood. Jesus goes on to demand exceptional righteousness as a precondition of entry into the kingdom (5:20) only, finally, to demonstrate what he has in mind by significantly raising the bar in several specific prescriptions. "You have heard it was said to those of ancient times . . . But I say to you . . ." He takes up anger, which he places side by side with murder, adultery through a mere roving gaze, divorce, oaths, forgiveness, and an extraordinary love of enemies.

It certainly goes to Luther's credit that, contrary to the interpretive tradition he himself was heir to, he sought to interpret the Sermon on the Mount as applicable in its entirety to all Christians. Luther, in fact, saw it as binding on all followers of Christ. There is no warrant, Luther insists on several occasions, to divide the Sermon into commands aimed at all Christians, on the one hand, and "evangelical counsels" that, on the other hand, are intended only for "those who want to become perfect, [counsels] to be kept by anyone who pleases."[9] Luther's broad application, however, must not imply that the Sermon does not call for interpretive discernment and nuance. As Luther sees it, we are required to distinguish—not between degrees of personal perfection we are willing to commit to, but between how we should act where our own status and affairs are at stake, where the Sermon's injunctions are very much apropos, versus how we ought to exercise responsibility for the security and well-being of our neighbor, where they are less so. In other words, as we approach the Sermon's injunctions, such as "Do not resist an evildoer" (5:39), we must recognize the difference between the ethical implications of freedom from oneself, as such, and how this freedom subsequently issues in freedom for the neighbor. Without compromising the Sermon's applicability, Luther's distinction allows him a degree of practical realism that reckons with sin and unbelief's sinister presence in the world, a presence that absolutely must be confronted on behalf of the neighbor. So interpreted, the Sermon enabled Luther to formulate his teaching about the

---

9. "The Sermon on the Mount," *LW* 21:4.

divine and secular realms, about temporal and spiritual authority.[10] All in all, although Luther certainly avoids reducing the Sermon to a matter of subjective feasibility or personal preference, the Sermon's applicability is subsumed under a strict criterion of self-reference and self-examination. Its thrust is deeply personal. More importantly still, so interpreted, the Sermon can be only law. Thoroughly appreciated, broadly, even if only personally, applicable, even foundational—but law all the same.

This preliminary foray into the Sermon on the Mount has allowed us to ask our own question of the text. It is now time that we allow the text not only to respond to our question but to speak directly to it, to question the question itself. It is not just a matter of asking in what way the Sermon on the Mount is law and gospel. Given how much the Sermon actually has to say about the law, it is difficult not to see the Sermon as a polemic about the law. Considering also the Speaker of the Sermon himself—the One who has come to fulfill the law—we would be remiss if we were to overlook how the Sermon informs our categories of law and gospel, how it addresses itself to their mutual interrelatedness, and how it ultimately speaks to what they are precisely in relation to each other.

The Sermon as Polemic About the Law

We begin with a fundamental, though only rarely explored, observation about the Preacher himself. In the Gospel according to Matthew, as in the other Synoptics, Jesus assumes the role of Israel.[11] Jesus' public ministry is inaugurated when he is baptized by John, anointed by the Spirit of God, and declared by "a voice from heaven" to be "my Son, the Beloved, with

---

10. "Temporal Authority: To What Extent It Should Be Obeyed," *LW* 45:75–129; for an engagement with the Sermon on the Mount, see esp. 81–90.

11. For the sake of clarity, this observation does not imply supersessionism. Rather, what it does convey is the *essential* role of Israel for understanding Jesus. Without Israel, or with Israel only a contingent keeper of divine promises concerning a redeemer but little more than that, Jesus can be only a gnostic savior figure, as the subsequent century will show. For the New Testament traditions, Jesus comes, first and foremost, to the lost sheep of Israel (10:6; 15:24) as Israel's messiah. In this role, he undertakes the task of repairing, as it were, and seeing through Israel's history with its God. Only with the kingdom breaking in for Israel, in their God-appointed role of a people for all peoples, can Jesus be said to be the Savior of all, Jew and gentile alike. By the time the Gospel according to Matthew was written much of this theological thinking had already been undertaken for the sake of Jewish-Christian and increasingly gentile-Christian congregations—even if many of the insights were soon to be misunderstood and effectively forfeited.

whom I am well pleased" (3:17). The Jordan is the Red Sea. As they crossed the Red Sea, the Hebrew slaves became a people, those whom God had already claimed as his "firstborn son" (Exod 4:22). Baby Jesus' return from Egypt—which Matthew glosses with God's words reported by the prophet Hosea, "out of Egypt I called my son" (Hos 11:1; Matt 2:15)—already anticipates Jesus' future role in place and for the sake of Israel. Following his baptism, Jesus is led by the Spirit into the wilderness to be tempted by the devil. The temptations that come at the end of the forty days are in essence the temptations that Israel itself faced, and succumbed to, in the course of the people's long walk with God. The temptations all revolve around not trusting in God's goodness, provision, care, and deliverance, and the seemingly justifiable need to take one's fate into one's own hands, to take care of oneself. In Jesus, history thus repeats itself. Only not! As the beloved Son with whom God is well pleased, Jesus sees Israel's history through as God's faithful covenant partner—even as, delivered into the hands of men (17:22), he also stands in place of Israel as the bearer of divine rejection.

But Matthew's Jesus is not only the people—faithful in their place and yet, at the cross, bearing the brunt of their unfaithfulness. When Matthew tells his readers that, as Jesus went into the wilderness, he fasted not only for forty days,[12] but for forty days *and nights* (4:2), and soon thereafter "went up the mountain" (5:1) to deliver a sermon full of teaching, the evangelist wants his readers to have in mind also another figure, that of Moses. Moses, too, had fasted for forty days and forty nights, as he was with God atop Mount Sinai and before he delivered God's "words of the covenant, the ten commandments" to the people (Exod 34:28).

However, even as we are to see Jesus in light of Moses, it is immediately clear Jesus is no mere go-between between Jahveh and the people. The distance that is emphasized in Exodus, with Jahveh descending upon Mount Sinai and the people at a remove, is closed in Jesus. Jesus is Immanuel (1:23), the Son of the Living God (16:16), as well as the people, as they should have been all along, led by the Spirit and fulfilling the law and the prophets. He is God and God's people, God and God's beloved Son, together, in an indissoluble unity. As a Mosaic figure Jesus thus paradoxically renders the figure of Moses superfluous. No go-between is necessary. In his allusion to—and simultaneous deconstruction of—Moses, Matthew thus invites us, rather provocatively, to see in the Sermon on the Mount

---

12. Compare Mark 1:13 and Luke 4:2. See also Dale C. Alison Jr., *The New Moses: A Matthean Typology* (Minneapolis: Fortress, 1993), 166.

a polemic. This polemic is not so much with, as over, Mosaic law. It is a struggle for its proper understanding.

Jesus, as Matthew portrays him, is aware of his role. At the conclusion of his discourse, Jesus emphasizes the foundational character of his teaching. None other will, in fact, do. "Everyone then who hears these words of mine and acts on them will be like a wise man who built his house on rock." To ignore Jesus' words can be only foolish (7:24–27). The crowds, Matthew does not fail to note, are appropriately left astounded, "for he taught them as one having authority, and not as their scribes" (7:29). Before we focus even more closely on the figure of Jesus and examine his teaching, let us first look in more detail at the hearers and, more generally, at the crowds that accompany Jesus at this early stage.

We should linger for a moment longer at the Sermon's end. Here we observe the desired impact of Jesus' words. It can give us a clue as to what his teaching aims to accomplish. What immediately follows the Sermon on the Mount in Matthew's Gospel is a string of healing miracles performed by Jesus. In the first, we see a desperate leper who approaches Jesus as his last and only hope. "Lord, if you choose, you can make me clean," he pleads (8:2). Jesus heals him and thereupon sends him to "show [himself] to the priest, and offer the gift that Moses commanded," and to do so, interestingly, "as a testimony to them" (8:4). The cured leper is sent off as a living witness to what truly matters; he thus personally, as it were, expresses Jesus' judgment on the prevalent *practice* of the law.

The next miracle is even more revealing. A centurion begs Jesus to heal his servant. Before Jesus does so, he commends the centurion publicly, and in a rather telling way, for his faith: "Truly I tell you [all], in no one in Israel have I found such faith. I tell you, many will come from east and west and will eat with Abraham and Isaac and Jacob in the kingdom of heaven, while the heirs of the kingdom will be thrown into the outer darkness" (8:10–12). Both miracles emphasize an unmediated relationship to Jesus and, by extension, to God—the kind of relationship that Jesus himself typifies in his own person. Any other gestures, such as satisfying a sacrificial prescription, are and should be inscribed into this larger relational context. What is at stake here is, of course, the law. For the leper, for whom Jesus is his last resort, it no longer comes into the picture, except after the healing. As a leper he is already outside the law, "outside the camp" (Lev 13:46), excluded from the community that defines itself and draws boundaries around itself by the law. For the centurion, the law is not in the picture at all.

For both figures, nothing stands any longer in the way of their realization that only a divine, or at least supernatural, action can help.

As we now move to the beginning of the Sermon, we notice that Jesus already presupposes this kind of direct relationship with himself and with God in the case of his hearers. To be sure, it is not immediately clear to whom the Sermon is addressed: some of the newly called disciples (5:1–2), or the great and rather diverse crowds that followed Jesus "from Galilee, the Decapolis, Jerusalem, Judea, and from beyond the Jordan" (4:25), or, even more remotely, the catechumens hearing Matthew's Gospel? In the end, it does not seem to matter. They are all alike fresh recipients of Jesus' mountaintop teaching. And so, it is all the more significant that right from the start they are called the salt and light of the world (5:13–16), warned about suffering persecution and bearing slander on Jesus' account, and even more so already blessed in advance. Blessed, for even though they may find themselves on the margins, they are already, perhaps unbeknownst to themselves, at the center of God's movement toward them, direct or indirect recipients of Jesus' summons, disciples-in-the-making and onlookers who no longer can be mere bystanders. To all of them, God already is father—"Our Father" (6:9)—not because they have already prayed to him but because they may approach God on his own account, because of who God is. All they can responsibly do is recognize what is the case: "Immanuel—God with us." As presupposing, and to some degree announcing, all this, the Sermon on the Mount is gospel. Its center is the living Good News himself, Jesus Christ, the beloved Son, thanks to whom others, too, are sons and daughters. It is from this center that the Sermon makes its argument about the law.

The Sermon's polemic proceeds on two tracks, as it were. Side by side we find two assertions that, at first glance, do not appear to sit well with each other. First, right after Jesus announces that he has not come to abolish the law but to fulfill it (more on this in a moment), he utters the following warning. "Whoever breaks one of the least of these commandments, and teaches others to do the same, will be called least in the kingdom of heaven; but whoever does them and teaches them will be called great in the kingdom of heaven" (5:19). Here Jesus' attitude to the law seems remarkably lenient. The coming kingdom of heaven has already embraced the hearers. Whether they keep or break the law, even deliberately break it, certainly matters; but it does not impinge on their standing in the kingdom. Fundamentally, it cannot be altered by them.

They can neither achieve it nor disavow it. They can only, as it were, move within the heavenly hierarchy of greatness. (We will have to say more to this apparent condoning of lawbreaking presently, as well.)

Now, just because our fundamental standing in the kingdom cannot be achieved or disavowed by us does not mean that *God himself* cannot determine one's inclusion or exclusion. He certainly can—and, importantly, he already has. But this inclusion, crucially, remains God's act alone. It emphatically cannot be taken over, naturalized, or secured post facto by one's own powers. Sonship is what it is only on account of the Father's renewed mercies. As Jesus will say later, "your heavenly Father knows" what you need; he is after all a giver of good things (6:32; 7:11). Jesus expresses this freedom of God's decision, the fact that it remains only God's own, in his second pronouncement, which, on the face of it, appears to be at odds with the one before. "I tell you, unless your righteousness exceeds that of the scribes and Pharisees, you will never enter the kingdom of heaven" (5:20). This warning is then followed by a string of dual statements where Jesus makes the law infinitely more demanding than it might seem at face value: "You have heard that it was said to those of ancient times . . . But I say to you . . ." Although this demand for extraordinary righteousness appears to contradict the leniency of God toward those who break his commandments, this is not really the case. Rather, Jesus' second demand identifies and at the same time disarms a problem created not so much by one's failure to live up to God's law but, instead, by the confidence which the law inspires when one does keep it.

There is an implicit polemic here with the scribes and Pharisees—the sects of Jesus' day—but in this way also and more importantly with the entire history of Israel recorded in its own Scriptures. For all their diversity, the Jewish sects of Jesus' day were, after all, but a logical product of that history. In a nutshell, the position that Jesus criticizes by heightening the law's demand is the danger that Israel had repeatedly faced since Sinai—the danger of seeking the people's identity in the law. God's presence and action were surely remembered and celebrated, but they were remembered and celebrated as effectively past. They had become a matter of cherished memory. Their present legacy was the law—the one thing the people believed themselves to be left with in the present. Consequently, in the present, one assured the survival of the people, among others, by dotting the i's and crossing the t's, publicly and for all to see. Thus understood, that is, on the basis of the law, identity cannot but lie in a set of common and publicly shared gestures. Jesus' admonitions that almsgiving, prayer, and fasting be done privately must be considered in this light. With his insistence that those are always seen by "your Father who sees in secret" (6:1–18), Jesus identifies the danger that the law poses. He, moreover, challenges the false temporality that the law seems to create. That which is at one's disposal is not the only reality that is present; and that which is not at one's disposal need not be either past or future. Jesus' ascent up the mountain to deliver his teaching is meant to make that point with particular force. The present is infinitely larger than what our action can grasp. It is, first and foremost, God's present: the *gift* of what otherwise is bygone, history repeating itself, time folded back on itself, only to commence yet again. Jesus going up the mountain. Another chance!

Jesus, significantly enough, articulates this temptation posed by the law not to the scribes and Pharisees (whether there were any left by the time the Gospel was written is debatable). He addresses his words to the hearers of the Sermon. It is to them, and to us, that he says, "unless your righteousness exceeds that of the scribes and Pharisees." With these words, aiming to make the law impossible, Jesus warns his listeners. He seeks to diffuse the temptation the law presents to repeat the failure of Israel: the people's failure to entrust themselves wholly to God's action on their behalf, their propensity to doubt the freedom of God's presence. By raising the bar to an arguably impossible standard, Jesus comments on a danger that the law—even his own teaching—presents to sinners. This danger is precisely the danger of the law as such, the law regarded as something abstract, unto itself, self-explanatory and self-evident, exhausting itself in itself; and so, the law detached from the reality of God's action, the law as it has effectively, de facto (even if not de jure), taken the place of the Lawgiver. The law where the Lawgiver and Teacher has been understood only in terms of his law and collapsed into it. The danger, to put it briefly, is that of defining oneself by a teaching, by affiliation.

When so interpreted, the Sermon on the Mount comes very close to the argument I believe the apostle Paul to be making in his Epistle to the Romans (which, of course, predates Matthew's Gospel). When Paul claims that "'no human being will be justified in [God's] sight' by deeds prescribed by the law, for through the law comes the knowledge of sin" (Rom 3:20), and when he argues, further, that "sin is not reckoned when there is no law" (Rom 5:13), he means the ease with which the law is, as it were, taken over and comes to replace the One who gave it or at least interposes itself as the mediator of the relationship between the people and their God. The law thus reveals sin not merely as we fall short of it but precisely in the real possibility that it creates of its being kept. The law has the capacity to obscure and set aside the One who gave it, or at best place him at the disposal of the keeper of the law. In this way, the law not only reveals our shortcomings but it also, rather underhandedly, may further exacerbate the depth of our alienation from God, our lack of trust, even in a context when the memory of God is ceaselessly invoked.

Jesus will not have his teaching detached from himself. "Unless your righteousness exceeds that of the scribes and Pharisees . . ." is meant to set aside for good the temptation that the law poses to the sinner to secure one's status. For one cannot be any more righteous than the Pharisees—unless one is righteous in an entirely different way, outside the law.

Righteousness and the Law

This brings us back to the figure of Jesus himself—his righteousness on our behalf and ours in light of his. At the Jordan, ignoring John the Baptist's protestations, Jesus submits to baptism, as administered by John, in order, as Matthew puts it, "to fulfill all righteousness" (3:15). At that moment the history of Israel is represented, repeated, and set in motion to be repaired. The crossing of the Red Sea made the Hebrew slaves, the nonentities that they were, into a people; Jesus ceases to be a private individual only to emerge from the waters of the Jordan as the Israelite for all Israel, a man through whom diverse crowds will be blessed, just as Israel was to have been a blessing to the nations and in Jesus became precisely that. Jesus emerges from Jordan's waters, above all, as the man who will live out of God's declaration, "This is my Son, the Beloved." He emerges from the waters of the Jordan as the man who does not let go of God's presence. From Jordan's banks, Jesus will be led into the wilderness, tempted, nevertheless, to take matters into his own hands, to doubt that God is with him or for him, to justify himself by his hunger, by his faith, by the urgency of his mission.[13] And some years later, in a moment of utter God-forsakenness (27:46), Jesus will once and for all do what the people repeatedly failed to do. He will stake his entire being,

---

13. For an insightful exegesis of the synoptic accounts of Jesus' temptation in the wilderness, not in terms of lawbreaking but in terms of self-justification, see Karl Barth, *Church Dogmatics* IV/1, trans. G. W. Bromiley (Edinburgh: T&T Clark, 1956), 259-83.

his identity as the Son, on the provision of the Father—even in the chill of the tomb and the silence that will come before Easter's dawn.

It is in this manner, with a whole life oriented to God's presence, that Jesus fulfills all righteousness and so also *fulfills* the law. It is already in his own person, as we have indicated before, that Jesus forecloses the possibility of the law's detachment from the Lawgiver. What was possible with Moses, though only as a faithless and senseless possibility, is no longer possible with Jesus. In Jesus, moreover, the Lawgiver and the people are joined together: God for his people and God's people before him. The law cannot be abstracted from this prior and overarching relationship as something to be kept in its own right. It is always the law of the living God who is present to his people in advance with all good gifts, not least the gift of himself. Jesus lives out this relationship of faithfulness, as he recapitulates before the Father the history of his people.

In this, Jesus cannot really be said to have kept the law. There is, after all, much he has no need or opportunity to keep. At any rate, even if he were to have kept it all, that would make him only an extraordinary Pharisee but would not, as such, reverse the sin-fraught history of Israel. Instead, Jesus fulfills the law and the prophets (*plēroō* rather than *fulassō*)—all of it—by according it its proper place in the inalienable context of God's presence, God's action, God's prior establishment of the person, and his summons of a people, as well as God's continued provision for his own. It is in this context that we must see Jesus' remarkable freedom within the law, his freedom for fellow humans, and hence his declaration that "the Son of Man is the Lord of the Sabbath" (12:8), and his concluding indictment of the Pharisees, in the last of the Matthean discourses, where Jesus accuses them of "neglect[ing] the weightier matters of the law: justice and mercy and faith" (23:23).

When it now comes to our righteousness, we must see it in light of Jesus and his freedom not so much from the law as within it. Only from this perspective can Jesus' words be made sense of: "Whoever breaks one of the least of these commandments, and teaches others to do the same, will be called least in the kingdom of heaven." Now, this certainly does not mean that we are free to break the law as we please! What it does mean, I believe, is that the law receives its perfection not through spiritualization, as if we really had to mean what we do (whatever that means!), heightening its demand, or being added to. Rather, the law achieves perfection in its personal exercise, for which the law actually calls. What is involved here is a prior personal relationship, an other-regard that is not created by the law but precedes it. The reason this matters is because the law, as such, is incapable of providing for every eventuality without degenerating into casuistry. However comprehensive, the law cannot, therefore, exempt and excuse us from seeing the other in the other's particularity, in his or her own unique plight. For this, if for no other, reason, the law should not be exploited as an instrument of judgment (7:1–5)—a rather blunt instrument in itself. Aristotle had already drawn attention to the fact that without equity (*epieikeia*) the law, understood in itself, as the impersonal letter, is incapable of achieving justice.[14] We need to be clear here. This does not mean that I am necessarily to take the other as the other understands himself or herself, to provide only what the other has deemed appropriate. This conclusion does not follow. What does follow is that my relationship to the other is not comprehended within the law but comes to inform how I go about it.

Now, and this is absolutely crucial, this kind of freedom within the law—a freedom not of lawbreaking but of justice and mercy and faith—is possible only when another has seen me in my own plight and withheld his judgment. What the Sermon on the Mount assures me about is precisely that God has already been good to me, that I—as the person I am—am invited to sit down and listen. Can I do the same to my brother and sister, even to the least of these? I certainly *may*![15]

This, finally, explains why the Sermon's preoccupation is not so much with specific rules or piling on laws. When all is said and done, the Sermon simply asks me where my treasure is and who is my master (6:19–21, 24). And it invites me into the presence of God—the Father who is for me, the Son who has fulfilled all righteousness, and the Spirit who drives demons away, opens up our lips, and ushers us into the kingdom (10:20; 12:28). In God's presence, I am reassured not to worry about myself (6:25–34) but also not to give up (7:7–11). In the end, the Sermon presents me with a vision of reality: that of Immanuel, God with us. And it invites me—it invites *us*!—to dream big, as we all "strive for the kingdom of God and his righteousness" (6:33), seeking it not in ourselves but in Jesus' presence with us until the end of the age.

---

14. See, e.g., *Nicomachean Ethics* 5.10. For a more in-depth discussion, see also my chapter, "The Law in the Lutheran Tradition," in Jonathan A. Linebaugh, ed., *God's Two Words* (Grand Rapids: Eerdmans, 2018), 15–44.

15. I articulate a similar interpersonal vision in my article "Justified for Good: Luther's Message for Late Modern Times," *Word and World* 37 (2017) 360–71.

Conclusion

In closing, let me reaffirm the following. The Sermon on the Mount belongs to the gospel as Matthew tells it. At its center stands—sits!—the living Good News: the One who is present with God's presence and who has been extraordinarily free for me. As such, the Sermon is to be seen as a defense of the gospel. It is a vigorous engagement with the law, not to abolish it, but for the sake of the gospel.

Luther's fear of making the Sermon into a blueprint for communal life stemmed from Anabaptist attempts to do just that. But, contrary to the realist position that Luther eventually ended up taking, the Sermon certainly invites us as the Christian community to live, and to do so publicly, out of a different set of givens from the world's own coordinates. As a polemic with the law for the sake of the gospel, the Sermon invites us to live by and out of God's presence instead of allowing our vision to be scaled back by the sheer inescapability of sin in the world. The Sermon's thrust is unabashedly communal—but, and this must be emphasized both contra Luther and the Anabaptists, it is a gospel thrust that, as such, challenges all legalisms, including turning the Sermon into a law that now comes to define us.

The Sermon's ethic is fundamentally a gospel ethic: it invites me to be who I already am because of Christ's summons; it invites me to be a person who belongs to the history that Christ has already seen through to a good end. This history, after all, already includes me. Even so, the Sermon calls me to be a doer of the law. But the law is always the law of the present Christ—a law which always asks, "Who is your master? And who is your neighbor? Who are the least of these?" The law is in no way an end in itself. For this reason, the Sermon, in fact, finally emphasizes my freedom within the law for my neighbor's sake.

The Sermon's vision thus certainly extends beyond what I can do as merely a private individual confronted with a world of sin and unbelief—a solitary, soul-searching believer hemmed in by practical realism. The Sermon's vision resolutely includes what *we* can do together if we all take the presence of God seriously, if we all believe that it is for us. No law can grasp this, for the law, at its best, always and only points beyond itself to the Lawgiver and his people. He says, "You have heard it was said to those of ancient times . . . But I say to you . . ." But that is not the final word. That is only the beginning. We must not rest on our laurels. But there is no need to fall apart in the face of tomorrow either (6:34). We are, rather, permitted to knock and seek and find. And then there is more, and more. For who can set a limit to the possibilities opened up by Christ's presence—the possibilities of mercy, and justice, and faith? The kind of faith that takes God at his word and, withholding judgment, makes more of the neighbor than the neighbor deserves.

The genius of the Sermon on the Mount, the reason why it eludes us, lies precisely in the fact that it means to be just the beginning—the beginning of Matthew's Gospel and, even more so, the beginning of our life in God and in the neighbor. The kingdom of heaven, to be sure, has come near. But we—we can never say *we* have arrived. Only a wide road takes one to one's journey's end in no time at all. For us, the winding path to the narrow gate continues, and each turn is full of surprises (7:13–14). In short, the Sermon is always beyond itself. Its meaning is always in the gospel. We should not be surprised it challenges us, frustrates us, seduces us, sucks us in, leaves us sleepless; but it also captivates us with its stark and simple beauty, its possibilities, its ever larger vision. It astonishes.

3

Reading the Sermon on the Mount in a Culture of Victimhood

David Cloutier

AT THE CENTER OF Christianity is a slain innocent victim, one whose death is caused by a conspiracy of temporal authorities working to animate a mob-like crowd. Stories bearing many resemblances to this one—stories reverencing victims harmed by loose alliances between powerful state authorities and the crowds—have in recent years achieved a status of high, arguably supreme, moral potency in our social discourse. How should Christians understand these convergences of moral imagination? How is the ethics of Jesus related to what has been dubbed "the moral culture of victimhood," in which the image of the suffering victim is meant to call forth urgent moral response?[1] In an attempt to say something new about a well-worn text, the Sermon on the Mount, I want to make this connection.

The connection is necessarily complex, not one of simple embrace or rejection. I came to this realization specifically while teaching Pope Benedict's *Caritas in Veritate*. I was trying to help our seminarians understand the pope's concept of the need for ordinary, everyday business and political

---

1. The spur for my thinking here is Bradley Campbell and Jason Manning, *The Rise of Victimhood Culture: Microaggressions, Safe Spaces, and the New Culture Wars* (Cham, Switz.: Palgrave Macmillan, 2018), a study by serious sociologists about the phenomena that have arisen in the past seven to eight years.

relationships to be infused with "quotas of gratuitousness"[2]—comparing this to John Paul's solidarity, and suggesting how both were trying to insert a "more-than-justice" element into social relationships. They are a kind of proactive compassion, a going-out to the other, that Francis's papacy has made even more vivid. This "more-than-justice" ideal is clearly crucial to the culture of victimhood—for example, the calls to deal with long-embedded systemic racism and with mass migration are not satisfied with basic procedural justice. Yet, as I was generating other examples for the students, I used the idea of "going the extra mile" at your job—doing more than you are required to do. When I did so, I remembered the context for this command in the Sermon on the Mount: when a member of the *occupying imperial forces* requisitions you to carry their baggage for a mile, carry it for two! This is "more than justice"—but most definitely *not* in a way that would satisfy the current moral culture of victimhood. We have two moral cultures who at their core agree in their insistence on social relations that go beyond justice—but clearly not in the same way.

To make this comparison, I will proceed in four parts. First, I want to articulate elements of the moral culture in question. Because it has often been characterized by polarizing tags (anti-racism, woke), a more careful understanding of its claims is very needed. Second, I want to place this moral culture in its appropriate historical context. The culture of victimhood is an emergent reality, and especially if Christians are to appreciate its positive elements, we need to see it as a response to genuine deficiencies in the predecessor cultures. Third, I will turn to the Sermon on the Mount itself, most importantly arguing for a certain reading of its *contents* in light of its overall *context*—this reading will make clear the common ground it has with victimhood culture. But finally, I will draw out three key differences in the Sermon's program, ones that shed light on and provide a better alternative to the dysfunctional elements of victimhood culture.

Defining the Moral Culture of the Moment

What is victimhood culture? As its name suggests, it *organizes the moral concerns and obligations of both individuals and communities around the*

---

2. Benedict XVI, *Caritas in Veritate*, Vatican, June 29, 2009, paras. 34–39; https://www.vatican.va/content/benedict-xvi/en/encyclicals/documents/hf_ben-xvi_enc_20090629_caritas-in-veritate.html.

sufferings of victims. But I want to disaggregate some of its features in order to better understand what is going on. I will list seven, relatively quickly.

First, this moral culture gets off the ground by drawing on a fundamental notion of *fairness* that is pervasive in American and larger Western culture, and indeed is maybe the most important moral narrative of progress in American history.[3] The history is one of facing and fighting discrimination, with Exhibit A as the rejection of African American slavery and of the ensuing discriminations manifest in Jim Crow segregation.[4] Even if victimhood culture is new, the old anchor claims against unfairness and discrimination remain foundational, especially for its broad acceptance; no one wants to be on the side of "bigotry" or "hate."

However, there is much more going on. A second element of the culture is that a person's *suffering itself is at the root of the moral claim*. For example, if a student is struggling and falling behind, the very existence of the struggle is sufficient to claim our attention and response. We don't stop and ask questions about "Is it their fault?" We can recognize this element in the good Samaritan parable, in which the simple recognition of the suffering man evokes compassion and active caring. Or we can imagine Francis's oft-quoted image of a "field hospital," in which pestering the patient about their cholesterol levels or obesity is not the first thing we should be doing when they are wounded. Thus, we might label this element "care for suffering first, ask questions later."

The moral claim of the suffering itself then requires attention to the question of what is meant by suffering. Here, a third element can be identified, connected with what Carl Trueman has recently called "the rise of psychological man." That is to say, suffering need not be a matter of physical or even economic harm or lack. Suffering comes from *any kind of slight of a person's inner expression* of identity.[5] Charles Taylor's early 1990s essay on

---

3. The only possible competing narrative is the economic progress narrative, which has struggled to be publicly persuasive over the past fifty years (except for a brief period in the 1990s), as the middle class has stagnated, community business stability has declined, and poverty has persisted.

4. While the early twentieth century had prominent social movements such as the Klan and progressive eugenicists, both of whom attempted to justify publicly various discriminations, postwar America largely lived into a broad consensus that such claims were not simply incorrect but reprehensible. Other groups, most especially women, had obviously different historical experiences, but generally drew on this same narrative of overcoming discrimination and unfairness.

5. As Trueman puts it, "Oppression involves making people feel bad about themselves, less than fully human, or preventing them from being outwardly that which they are

"the politics of recognition" noted how this element of *interior identity recognition and affirmation* constituted a different sort of moral language than did the earlier language of equal civil rights. While both languages emphasized that there were no second-class citizens, what it meant to be marginalized shifted: instead of access to "an *identical* basket of rights and immunities . . . what we are asked to recognize is the *unique* identity of this individual or group, their distinctiveness from everyone else."[6] Any deviation from this recognition causes victimization, and therefore suffering.[7]

A fourth element builds further: the moral responsibility toward victims involves not simply addressing their suffering but actively *preventing* it from happening in the first place. This makes sense when aimed at traditional forms of discrimination and violence, but, when combined with element 3 above, can lead to what one recent book called "safetyism," built on the myth that "what doesn't kill you makes you weaker."[8] Questions are continually debated about the moral responsibility implied, all of which typically hinge on how far to restrict individual freedoms in the pursuit of preventing bad things from happening, a question that ended up taking on immense conflictual value in the unexpected circumstances of the pandemic. Sensible questions about rational prevention strategies seemed swamped from both sides.

---

inwardly." Carl R. Trueman, "The Impact of Psychological Man—and How to Respond," *Public Discourse*, Nov. 10, 2020, para. 2; www.thepublicdiscourse.com/2020/11/72190/.

6. Charles Taylor, "The Politics of Recognition," in *Multiculturalism*, ed. Amy Gutmann (Princeton, NJ: Princeton University Press, 1994), 25–74, at 38; emphasis added.

7. There is a wide range of examples. For example, widespread concern about the harm caused by the use of cultural stereotyping is seen in concern over Native American sports team mascots. Or claims about "micro-aggressions" are the center of Campbell and Manning's sociological studies. These "brief and commonplace daily verbal, behavioral, and environmental indignities" are not connected to threats of physical violence or job loss, nor need they be intentional. But they serve to single out and thus harm individuals or groups—for example, difficulties in pronouncing unfamiliar names from certain cultures or being specially observed when entering a store. Campbell and Manning, *Rise of Victimhood Culture*, 3–4, quoting Derald Wing Sue. In yet another vein, key to issues such as marriage equality, transgender pronouns, and the multiplying sorts of gender identities is the concern to erase any sense of norm deviation from these expressions of inner feelings about one's sexuality. To be mis-pronounced is to be harmed and become a victim, just as in past days a racial slur might have been perceived as damaging.

8. For this problem and the "three great untruths" about human persons lying behind it, see psychologists Greg Lukianoff and Jonathan Haidt, *The Coddling of the American Mind* (New York: Penguin, 2018).

The fifth element adds membership in a particular *group* as evidence of victimhood; individual victim stories are exemplary of larger structural injustices against groups, in which all members are victims. This is important to highlight as a distinctive element because in examples like the good Samaritan or the struggling student, this group element is not necessarily present. The Samaritan, after all, is not the one by the side of the road! This group element often transforms the above elements. For example, the assumption of suffering by all members of a victimized group, combined with the demands for prevention of suffering (element 4), lead to the need to demonstrate equal group outcomes in light of the imperative to address suffering without asking about causes (element 2).[9]

The sense of group victimization is then increased by a sixth element, which is an appeal to inerasable *historical* injustices against a given group. Here we move another step further from the man actually suffering at the side of the road to victimhood characterized by membership in a group that was subject to historical discrimination. Facing this conundrum, French philosopher Pierre Manent noted recently in an interview that "penance—which is less and less exacted in Christian churches—has found a very hospitable home in the political realm, except in the latter there is no absolution. Sin with neither responsibility . . . nor redemption."[10]

---

9. This strong shift to attributing unequal group outcomes to systemic causes that the society has a moral responsibility to address cannot be overestimated. For example, in the 2019 article titled with the splendid construction "The Great Awokening," Matthew Yglesias explains that, as late as 2014, polls suggested the majority of Americans believed the country had largely addressed discrimination between blacks and whites. Today, the number who see racial discrimination as an ongoing problem is much higher and, as Yglesias shows, is powered largely by a shift among white liberals, who now hold views about systemic discrimination that are to the left of African Americans and Hispanics. In Yglesias's words, "White liberals are now *less* likely than African Americans to say that black people should be able to get ahead without any special help" (*Vox*, Apr. 1, 2019, s.vv. "Democrats have become more liberal on race questions"; https://www.vox.com/2019/3/22/18259865/great-awokening-white-liberals-race-polling-trump-2020).

10. Nathaniel Peters, "Europe and America after COVID: An Interview with Pierre Manent," *Public Discourse*, June 12, 2021, para. 15; https://www.thepublicdiscourse.com/2021/06/76281/. Manent also notes that any serious examination of conscience for sins of the historical past cannot be a partisan enterprise (final para.). The focus on historical injustice may also come from the fact that overt expression of overall "racial and sexual prejudice" has been decreasing steadily for decades in the US. For data and an analysis of the paradoxical rise in the use of certain language about oppression in the news media, see David Rozado, "Prejudice and Victimization Themes in *New York Times* Discourse: A Chronological Analysis," *Academic Questions* 33 (2020) 89–100.

A final element to note is the centrality of *third-party appeals*. At the root of this element is the notion that victims have been robbed of their voices, and so now they have an obligation to "speak up" and others have an obligation to hear them. Third-party appeals are part of a larger trend in the burgeoning academic field of "victimology" that stress how victims themselves are not just passive; as one collection of papers on the topic indicate, they have agency, especially in constructing and ritualizing their status as victims through various cultural practices.[11] Such appeals force individuals and institutions into a "for-us-or-against-us" posture in relation to victims. In order to manage the (clearly unruly) process of third-party appeals, institutions subject themselves to various bureaucratic structures whose purpose is to police their members for potential offenses. Social media has amplified this third-party-appeal process enormously.[12] Appealing to the Twitter mob is the quintessential third-party appeal, and institutions have to spring into (very quick) action when exposed by a particular individual action.

The Emergence of Victimhood Culture

Disaggregating these elements helps us get a handle on what we are talking about, but we also need to understand victimhood culture historically. Victimhood culture does not come out of nowhere. Manning and Campbell argue that it emerges out of a predecessor "moral culture of dignity."[13] The hallmark of their explanation of dignity culture is a sense that the worth of a person arises from within, that their worth is *inherent*, rather than dependent on reputational variables. "Sticks and stones may

11. Martin Hoondert et al., "Introduction," in *Cultural Practices of Victimhood*, ed. Martin Hoondert et al., Victims, Culture and Society (London: Routledge, 2019), 3.

12. Such structures then have to identify offenders and subject them to public penalty, a necessary way of responding to the third-party appeal but also an effective way of saying to other members of the organization, "Be careful not to do anything that will provoke a third-party appeal." The centrality of third-party appeals to the current moral culture is inseparable from the characteristics of social media—the instantaneous and anti-institutional elements of this media make third-party appeals unusually easy and powerful. Yglesias's article also suggests that the shift in white liberal views has a lot to do with social media and how particular events became magnified by certain dynamics of the new media. But I would add it's not simply that events like police violence became newly visible and prominent because of social media technologies; it's also the case that more and more events demanded quick and decisive signaling by others on social media.

13. Campbell and Manning, *Rise of Victimhood Culture*, 12–16.

break my bones, but names will never hurt me" is a quintessential expression of a dignity culture.

The authors explain how dignity culture emerges out of yet another moral culture, of "honor." Dignity culture's tendency to minimize reactions to slights, develop thick skins, and resolve conflicts privately are all strong contrasts to honor culture. But the even deeper and more fundamental contrast is where personal value lies: routinely, the proper honor involves belonging to some kind of social group or class, whereas dignity culture (at least over time) assumed dignity to mean a basic level of respect due to all, regardless of their position or group.

The dignity/honor contrast, however, also helps us see how victimhood culture emerges because of certain deficiencies in dignity culture. A dignity culture, for example, might encourage women and children to tolerate abusive behavior or handle such things only behind closed doors. It might fail to understand why third-party systems are important, a key failing in the Catholic clergy sexual abuse crisis. Perhaps most importantly for Christians, dignity cultures encourage a kind of self-reliance and independence that not only discourage people from asking for help when they need it, but also discourage active recognition that what we owe to others is not simply to let them be (or to let them be cared for by "someone else"). Dignity cultures may reduce conflict, but they also may reduce interdependence.

The limitations of dignity cultures are even more apparent insofar as they move in more and more individualist directions. This is the key claim of my paper: the moral concerns of victimhood culture are best understood as a substitute language for civic and Christian social concerns, as more traditional versions of civic and Christian languages decay, and (as a consequence) unadorned dignity culture becomes more and more individualistic. At least in the US, communitarian dignity cultures[14] like unions or African American churches faced severe headwinds, on the Left from a 1960s movement toward individual expressivism in culture, on the Right from a 1980s movement toward free market competition and global trade, and on both sides from the geographical shift to suburbia. This shift toward individualism meant that dignity cultures left a smaller and smaller space for articulating social responsibility; and further, dignity culture's disdain

---

14. Mark Lilla refers to these as "the Roosevelt dispensation" in his book, critiquing victimhood culture, *The Once and Future Liberal: After Identity Politics* (New York: HarperCollins, 2017).

for hereditary aristocracies easily leads to the alternative: some sort of meritocracy.[15] People succeed or fail because they deserve it—any remaining suffering, and there was still plenty, must be these people's own fault. While dignity cultures do not need to be individualistic, in the absence of other communal forces, they tend to become "stand-on-your-own-two-feet" culture—where if you sink, it's your own fault.

What happened? I think the key to the rise of victimhood moral culture is what we might call the "slow retirement" of moral languages that mitigated the individualism of dignity culture. In *Habits of the Heart*, Robert Bellah and his associates identified these mitigating languages as the cultural languages of biblical religion and classical republicanism.[16] Bellah's study is not simply a period piece; it is clearer now that they were correct to identify the decay of biblical and republican languages as the key turning moment of the time. These languages, embedded in practices of church and town,[17] provided a longtime counterweight that inhibited Alexis de Tocqueville's worries about American "individualism." They enabled the formation of commitments to others and oriented people toward larger identities in which they felt ownership, they encouraged all sorts of pro-social, mutually supportive activity, and they provided people with ways of dealing with guilt and death. This latter point might only be associated with church, but visiting any American town of a certain age, one cannot but be struck by the efforts made to memorialize things.

---

15. The prevalence of current critiques of meritocracy sometimes misses the idea that meritocracy is meant to be an alternative to systems of group privilege, nepotism, and the like. Thus, whatever its weaknesses, the meritocratic elements of civil service examinations, scientifically demanding professions, and the like clearly do provide some considerable social benefits. It seems to me the critiques of meritocracy would be better leveled at either (a) how pervasive it has become (e.g., youth sports) or (b) how the determination of "merit" is much more dubious in some areas compared to others.

16. Robert Bellah et al., *Habits of the Heart: Individualism and Commitment in American Life* (Berkeley: University of California Press, 1985), 28–31.

17. The notion of "the town" plays a notably central role in Bellah's story (e.g., *Habits*, 39) insofar as the town was the place where American farmers and craftsmen who "worked for themselves" nevertheless built a common life of associational institutions. Ben Sasse recently confronted this issue (*Them: Why We Hate Each Other and How to Heal* [New York: St. Martin's, 2018]) and has explained that when Americans migrated to cities, they ended up building neighborhoods that retained many elements of "town" life, but that various forces over the past two generations have led to a far more separated existence—not simply for the lonely individual, but for interactions to be mediated by professions and activist organizations that fail to convene the face-to-face variety of a town.

What they didn't anticipate—but what I think we now see—is that once these languages became more and more "minority languages," there would need to be substitute languages that would do at least some of the work these older languages did. I think at some (obviously non-exact) point, there was a kind of tipping point, where these languages—as languages that could be used in common—simply ended up failing.[18] A pretty big void opened up, and it largely opened up on the Left. As someone who went to (and loved) an elite, small liberal arts college in the early 1990s, you might say I saw the leading edge of this. Carleton College was a fantastic community, but neither American citizenship identification nor Christianity were languages that united the community any longer.[19] There were just residues, and this already left some looking around for a stronger language of civic commitment.

Thus, my larger point: the moral culture of victimhood is filling a gap left by the limits of an individualist dignity culture. It is attempting to

---

18. Alternatively, the languages of civic pride and Christianity went from being unifying languages to specifically partisan languages. James Davison Hunter's *Culture Wars: The Struggle to Define America* (San Francisco: Basic/HarperCollins, 1991) explains that, especially from the late nineteenth century through the early postwar period, the language of "biblical theism" provided a "cultural cement," offering common imagery to Jews, Catholics, and Protestants to generate a shared understanding of the American project. Dividedness actually diminished, and even the great racial divide could be bridged by drawing on this common language. Yet over time, "parallel fissures" opened up within each of these groups, as "special agenda" groups started publicly advocating for quite different civic projects, most especially with those claiming languages of traditional religious authority against certain changes. The effect was to subordinate the common language to partisan agendas and, over time, to sort the more overtly biblical language on the conservative side. Just as I was completing the paper, a new volume of rigorous political science (David E. Campbell et al., *Secular Surge: A New Fault Line in American Politics*, Cambridge Studies in Social Theory, Religion and Politics [New York: Cambridge University Press, 2020]) goes beyond traditional self-reports about affiliation to explore how pervasive a nonreligious worldview has become—by their measure, 43 percent of Americans are either nonreligious or actively secularist in their worldview, and their deeper survey of activists showed the dominance of the actively secular worldview among Democratic party activists, especially whites. Almost all party activists left who have any sort of religious worldview are African American or Hispanic.

19. The chapel and chaplain remained and a flag was hoisted on Willis Hall at the center of campus, but insofar as there was a common language, it was our own little civic experience on the tight-knit campus, a good bit of pop culture (which of course for us Gen Xers still had the older stuff sprinkled in it), and a certain sense of make-the-world-better intuitions. If anything, the dominant, unquestioned moral language was that of freedom and authenticity, a language that resonated with the astonishing larger events of the fall of the Soviet bloc.

provide some of the civic commitment and transcendent meaning that was formerly supplied by certain practices of engaged citizenship and certain deep moral beliefs about right and wrong drawn from Christianity. As Tara Isabella Burton argues, it is the prime candidate for a new comprehensive civil religion, insofar as it "provides both an explanation for evil" and "a language, symbol set, and collection of rituals" with which to combat it.[20] Victimhood culture emerges in exactly the cultural space—elite institutions, largely on the political Left—where Christian and traditional civic appeals decayed the most rapidly. Overall, then, it's not so much that dignity culture is simply *replaced* by victimhood culture, but rather that victimhood culture emerges out of the prior cultural matrix to fill a Christian-shaped gap.

The Sermon on the Mount as a Program of Social Initiative

What does all of this have to do with the Sermon on the Mount? Of course, it would be wrong to say that Bellah's biblical strand was actually people living out the Sermon! Like some forms of Marxist liberationism, what in fact we get in aspects of the culture of victimhood is a Christianity that puts to shame existing Christianity. As Joseph Ratzinger once wrote about liberation theology, the aspects he judged pernicious and misguided "would not have been able to wrench that piece of the truth to its own use if that truth had been adequately lived and witnessed to in its proper place (in the faith of the church)."[21] So when we hear that those who mourn are

---

20. Tara Isabella Burton, *Strange Rites* (New York: PublicAffairs, 2020), quoted in Bradley Campbell, "What the Right Gets Wrong About Social Justice Culture," *Quillette*, July 20, 2020, s.vv. "Social justice culture as religion"; https://quillette.com/2020/07/20/what-the-right-gets-wrong-about-social-justice-culture/. Campbell's piece accepts this conclusion that the default path forward will be this new civil religion, unless and insofar a more compelling alternative contends for the field. For more on Burton, listen to this podcast interview with Russell Moore: "A Conversation with Dr. Tara Isabella Burton About Strange Rites," *The Russell Moore Show*, May 5, 2021; https://www.russellmoore.com/2021/05/05/a-conversation-with-dr-tara-isabella-burton-about-strange-rites/. A further reason to support this view of the new post-Christian civil religion is the observation of Campbell and Manning that the historical emergence of this culture is clearly among elites, but now trickling "down" into the culture; they note that dignity culture interestingly originated in the opposite direction, as middling classes sought to resist aristocratic elites. See Claire Lehmann's perceptive review of their victimhood culture book in *Commentary* (June 2018) 53–55.

21. Benedict XVI, "Liberation Theology," in *The Essential Pope Benedict XVI*, ed. John Thornton and Susan Varenne (New York: HarperOne, 2007), 217–25, at 217.

blessed, we might think of the memorials to those who have lost their lives in police shootings. When we hear those who hunger and thirst for righteousness are blessed, we should think how single-minded and committed many are to this cause. They "seek it first"!

Yet, as I indicated at the beginning, some elements of the same Sermon appear about as incompatible with the moral culture as could be. "Go the extra mile" refers to enforced carrying of the gear of Roman officials. "Not getting angry" might well look like complicity with the oppressors, or even a command that is a form of violence itself. Making one's pious action visible (rather than doing it in secret) is absolutely essential for victims and their allies. And of course loving enemies and forgiving others as we expect to be forgiven do not seem to be part of the program.

In this context, I assume all are familiar with the contents of the Sermon. So my task here is to ask about the *whole* Sermon—not the Sermon as a free-standing set of moral observations, as if treating a résumé of Jesus' memes or tweets, but as an overall discourse that emerges from and responds to a particular social situation. I then want to take those observations about the *whole* Sermon and, as William Spohn put it, "spot the rhyme"[22]—show how *the content of the Sermon in context relates to the content of the culture of victimhood in its context*. This relation will help us see both the common ground and the key differences.

I do not want to belabor obvious points about the Sermon. Still, it's important to point out that the Sermon must be read in the context of the presentation of Jesus as the *Jewish* Messiah. In this sense, everything Jesus does is a commentary on the situation of first-century Jews in relation to God's promises. So, while I of course agree with St. Augustine that the Sermon is "the charter of the Christian life," it is important to see it first as a charter for *Jewish* life! This charter exists in its context in relation to (at least) three other Israel projects: the Pharisees, those who advocate retreat into secluded communities, and those who advocate and/or expect armed rebellion against the Romans.

In the Sermon, Jesus is not offering a call to arms or a retreat from society. Definitely not. The extent to which the first option could have been expected is brought home to me often when I pray the psalms, which have no difficulty at all petitioning God to bring down all sorts of bad things on Israel's enemies. Israel's history would have given them

---

22. William Spohn, *Go and Do Likewise: Jesus and Ethics* (New York: Continuum, 1999), 54–56.

every reason to expect that the promised leader would in fact be a successful (or at least subversive) military leader. Jesus could not have given more contrary direction. Yet neither is there a call to retreat from society. Instead, there is a focus on visible, faithful practice (e.g., the light and salt metaphors)—albeit a rather different visible, faithful practice than that of the Pharisees. Matthew's well-known harshness toward the Pharisees is likely a sign that their program was *close* to Jesus' own, but crucially different in ways that should be highlighted.

In that context of competing programs, I think Glen Stassen and David Gushee's proposal of understanding the overall Sermon in terms of *socially transformative initiatives* is extremely helpful.[23] This is the key "rhyme" that I want to hold up: characteristic of the moral culture of victimhood is not simply social transformation, but the *imperative* to take up responsibility actively for that transformation. To initiate. So too should we understand the Sermon on the Mount.

Stassen and Gushee propose this approach especially as an alternative way of reading the "antitheses." Instead of seeing them in two parts, they suggest three—a hypothetical saying, a recognition of that saying's creation of a "violent cycle," and then a command to do something different. In making this proposal, they are trying to avoid a set of common misreadings of the whole document—ones that interiorize it, make it into a high but impossible ideal, or attempt to read this explicitly and literally as a new code. Instead, the focus is (in every case) breaking a cycle. This reading is most obvious in the sayings about anger and about the *lex talionis*, where there is explicitly reference to the sort of cycle that underlies the literal obedience of the hypothetical (common-sense!) saying. But the reading opens up good ways of understanding other antitheses as well. For example, a cultural commitment to oath swearing can develop all sorts of ways to evade truth telling, whether in legal culture or in corporate speak; we accept it all too easily in advertising and public relations. And as our culture sadly depicts, a correct rejection of destructive and violent sexual actions is very difficult to square with a pornographic habit of mind.

This reading helps us take the Sermon quite *seriously*, without imagining that it is meant to lay out a *code*. The tendency to consider the Sermon as a straightforward code is a key reason why historical debates over its reception get so hung on whether it is "possible" or "impossible." My

---

23. Glen H. Stassen and David P. Gushee, *Kingdom Ethics: Following Jesus in Contemporary Context* (Downers Grove, IL: InterVarsity, 2003), 128–43.

colleague at CUA, Ian Boxall, has recently published a fantastic reception history of Matthew's Gospel, and his section on the reception of the Sermon displays how a key concern has always been the "difficulty" question. This is especially true after the Reformation, but Boxall nicely notes that even the Didache seems to recognize that this is not possible for all, and early manuscripts themselves evidence the addition of "without cause" to the command not to get angry.[24]

Even from historical context, there is good reason to adopt this reading. As Richard Hays puts it, quoting Wayne Meeks, the rules of the Sermon are meant to be "exemplary not comprehensive," and this can be seen in contrast with the much more exhaustive approaches of other Jewish communities of the time, in the Mishnah and at Qumran, for example.[25] We can also understand this reading of the Sermon by means of Pope Francis's explanation of the contrast between "controlling spaces" versus "initiating processes."[26] He uses this contrast especially imaginatively in a section of *Amoris Laetitia* about parenting. He insists that parents "know where their children are," but contrasts "knowing" in a helicopter-parent, controlling sort of way versus being able to travel with them and know "where they are existentially, where they stand in terms of their convictions, goals, desires, and dreams." Parents who monitor their children physically are worried about control and domination, Francis says, not about "starting processes" that will "help [children] grow in freedom, maturity, overall discipline, and real autonomy."[27]

What kinds of initiatives or processes are being envisioned by the Sermon? Well, there is not just one. For example, the section on prayer, fasting, and almsgiving clearly takes on the temptations to imagine these practices as public shows. The initiative is also clear: do these things in secret. Here already we have an interesting conversation with the contemporary

---

24. Ian Boxall, *Matthew Through the Centuries* (Oxford: Wiley/Blackwell, 2018), 99–149.

25. Wayne Meeks, *The Origins of Christian Morality* (New Haven, CT: Yale University Press, 1993), 140, quoted in Richard Hays, *The Moral Vision of the New Testament* (San Francisco: HarperCollins, 1996), 98.

26. This is the meaning of his programmatic aphorism "time is greater than space." Francis, *Evangelii Gaudium*, Vatican, Nov. 24, 2013, paras. 222–25; https://www.vatican.va/content/francesco/en/apost_exhortations/documents/papa-francesco_esortazione-ap_20131124_evangelii-gaudium.html.

27. Francis, *Amoris Laetitia*, Vatican, Mar. 19, 2016, paras. 260–62; https://www.vatican.va/content/dam/francesco/pdf/apost_exhortations/documents/papa-francesco_esortazione-ap_20160319_amoris-laetitia_en.pdf.

victimhood cultural norm: "When you do some good deed, make sure everyone on Twitter knows exactly what you are doing . . . and change your Facebook photo while you're at it . . . oh, and put it on your lawn."

But as I've said all along, the point here is to see that Christianity and this moral culture are not so much pure contrasts as they are quite *closely related* programs in which some significant things are in common, but with some decisive differences in the overall package. The point is not to impose a norm of secrecy on institutional initiatives, but to ask what prompts the different concerns of the Sermon (for invisibility, at least on these things) and the current culture (for visibility).

Yet before taking on those deeper contrasts, it's really important not to miss the key shared territory. Gerhard Lohfink's treatment of the Sermon is particularly compact and compelling: the call of the gospel is *a call for a new family (which is the reunited Israel initially) that is especially committed to giving up relationships of violence and domination, in light of the single authority of God*.[28] This isn't just dignity-culture-style "love your neighbor—no exceptions." What this approach adds is a recognition of the (many) ways in which that love is an *active* one, within and outside the Christian community. It is a love that takes initiatives to transform particular relationships of domination. Lohfink, for example, notes the command in another Matthean discourse to go out without staff (the wanderer's defense) and sandals (the wanderer's ability to flee danger) as "a demonstrative signal of the absolute readiness for peace."[29] Of course, love your enemy is the quintessential expression of this aim.

Lohfink's argument is strengthened by his paralleling of the ethic of the Sermon with the work of the Spirit in the post-resurrection New Testament communities. After the resurrection, and especially in the mission to the gentiles, the work of the Spirit is in case after case a matter of breaking through and overcoming various barriers and (subsequently) living in harmonious, reconciling ways with one another.[30] Once one sees this, it is really striking how many different aspects of Pauline ethics can be seen as basically this constant pushback against division and conflict, and in particular, ways of practicing that may seem zealous and faith filled

---

28. Gerhard Lohfink, *Jesus and Community: The Social Dimension of Christian Faith*, trans. John P. Galvin (Philadelphia: Fortress, 1984), 39–72.

29. Lohfink, *Jesus and Community*, 54. This single authority is articulated in different ways (e.g., seek first the kingdom of God, do the will of God), but is most importantly condensed in the word "father."

30. Lohfink, *Jesus and Community*, 81–122.

but are in fact misguided (e.g., the idol meat case), in fact divisive, and eventually cause domination.[31]

If we accept that the core content of the Sermon is really about a contrast between relations of conflict and domination with a way of peace and reconciliation, and the further call to take active initiative to overcome the existing dynamics of domination, we will see that the shared terrain with the moral culture of victimhood is substantial indeed. While it's important not to minimize the extent to which dignity cultures did bring about a considerable degree of social pacification and diminishment of violence,[32] the Sermon's key alliance with victimhood culture is an insistence on *initiative*, rather than mere passivity. A certain kind of initiative. The insistence on showing mercy, hungering for righteousness, making peace, suffering for the sake of Christ—these all show initiative, more initiative certainly

---

31. For those interested, the parallel of the new law of the Sermon and the work of the Holy Spirit in Paul is nicely reflected in Aquinas's treatment in the *Summa* of "the new law" as centrally about the Holy Spirit, but also secondarily a written law (e.g., I-II, q. 106, a. 1).

32. The claim, made most forcefully in the public sphere by Steven Pinker (*Enlightenment Now* [New York: Penguin, 2018]), is that the moral culture of the Enlightenment—the dignity culture—has in fact produced the most nonviolent societies and world that we have ever seen. Pinker shares the typical Enlightenment suspicion of religious violence but also finds identity politics dangerous for some of the same reasons, its irrationality, partiality, and dogmatism. Pinker's claim is complicated. Enlightenment societies also explicitly produced nineteenth-century colonialism and the twentieth century's two most bloody conflicts. There is some reason to imagine that the Enlightenment's (relative) nonviolence is due more to a shift to *doux commerce* and the discovery of fossil fuel sources of energy, both of which create their own sets of problems! And, as we have already seen in Bellah, it's not clear that a solely modern sense of the self based on dignity can be sustained in social relationships without other ideas about community, especially transcendent community. Yet we should also be clear: Pinker is right to note the level of personal safety in pluralistic societies, for example, and the general (not total) fairness of public organizations. There is a real restraint of vendetta-style vengeance, a sense of truthful straightforwardness in speech, a dignity for women. There is even a sense of mercy in punishment incorporated in the gradual elimination of the death penalty, rights for criminals, and "anything that looked like extravagance in sanctions or penalties," which Oliver O'Donovan notes as an aspect of the Christian restraint on final judgment and that has proven fully compatible with dignity cultures that have rebelled against cruel and unusual punishments (*The Desire of the Nations* [New York: Cambridge University Press, 1996], 260). All incomplete, but all real. Thus, the Sermon can invite us to acknowledge the real success of dignity cultures . . . while also seeing all too plainly how limited that "success" is. Is the personal safety ultimately backed up by security cameras and the actionable threats of bombs and police, for example? Does it seal off sectors of society that can't be pacified, simply keeping them contained? Does it ignore the violence involved in publicly accepted spheres of sexual lust and untruthful speech?

than I habitually show in my daily life. And certainly more initiative than I and many other Christians show in addressing the continued suffering of so many people. This broad notion—John Paul called it solidarity, saying "we are all really responsible for all"[33]—is daunting.

The Differences the Sermon Highlights

But what exactly does "responsibility" entail? What are the initiatives, and why these? Here, we see where the Sermon and victimhood culture diverge. When asking what the *aim* of the moral culture of victimhood is—what is the social vision—it is hard to tell.[34] It seems animated either by what Taylor identifies as the key modern moral imperative of simply ending all suffering or by the more Marxian goal of removing the inherent oppressor class and replacing them in power. Both of these teloi are a bit shrouded in the present discourse, but in either case, Christians have a stake in saying bluntly: ending suffering per se is impossible and replacing one group in power with another does not solve the more fundamental problem. Simply replacing one power group with another will not end relations of domination, and preventing all suffering would require intolerable limitations on human freedom . . . and even then, might be impossible.

So what is the goal of the Sermon's initiatives? The goal is the daily discipline of practicing life in ways that open relationships broken by domination to transformation. Surely victimhood culture would agree, but here's a difference: they continue to use macrostructural tools to solve microstructural problems. One can imagine using nation-state politics and legal enforcement structures to end discrimination in public accommodations or denial of basic voting rights. But it is much harder to deal with the

---

33. John Paul II, *Sollicitudo Rei Socialis*, Vatican, Dec. 30, 1987, para. 38; https://www.vatican.va/content/john-paul-ii/en/encyclicals/documents/hf_jp-ii_enc_30121987_sollicitudo-rei-socialis.html.

34. Interestingly, Stassen and Gushee, writing in 2003, contrast the rural Tennessee town in which one of them teaches with the diverse, prosperous, intermarrying population of the northern Virginia suburbs of DC (*Kingdom Ethics*, 405). For its time, this is a conventional vision, but of course now, the NoVa suburbs are animated by strident calls to overcome systemic racism within those very communities, in the schools, in policing, in housing policy, and in drug laws, to name only a few. Stassen and Gushee articulate what might have been a commonplace in 2003 about where this led: nonsegregated cultural spaces that were at ease with people with different skin colors and ethnic heritages, in which family formation then began to melt and blend these into one richer whole.

rest of the problem—at the legal level, you can establish some outer bounds of justice, but then the real micro-level work must begin.

And at this micro level, the Sermon succeeds brilliantly, in contrast to some of the most problematic aspects of victimhood culture. I will approach this by identifying three things the Sermon has but the existing, dominant discourse of victimhood culture does not have, identifying one springboard text off of which one can speak of particular challenges to the contemporary culture.

The first point is to make clear that the peaceable ethics of the Sermon depends on God. The crucial text here is, in my opinion, the hardest of all the sayings in the Sermon: the one about the lilies of the field. The bluntness of Jesus' saying, correlating to the prayer in the Our Father for "daily bread," means a constant reliance on God's providence, on the God who makes the rains fall on the just and the unjust. Without God—and without the sort of God revealed in Jesus and the Sermon—the whole peacemaking thing is crazy. God matters, and insofar as any discourse of victimhood culture is godless, it goes wrong. Note that this does not mean there needs to be a chaplain-like benediction at the beginning of the protest march. The ultimate reliance on providence here is "not of this world," even though it is clearly in the world. This difference God makes needs not so much to be *stated* as to be *explained*. This is ultimately a trust in the unity of the human race; a refusal especially to imagine the human world as inherently divided and conflictual, but as one under God. The love of enemies is a matter of the transcendent, loving Lord of all—it is not a denial that there are enemies, but a claim about how to understand those enemies in the context of God's care for all creation.

But the difference God makes is also a matter of getting the self right. I previously noted the aspect of victimhood culture in which one's inner sense of identity must be recognized and affirmed. But the very idea of an inner sense of identity itself goes back to the personal God of Christianity. Francis Fukuyama traces this notion of inner identity as all important and anchored in God over against external social identification to Luther, but notes that Luther's sense of the inner self not only "did not seek public recognition" but also was a matter of faith in God's grace (or a lack of such faith).[35] Indeed, the fundamental identification of the self was as a

---

35. Francis Fukuyama, *Identity: The Demand for Dignity and the Politics of Resentment* (New York: Farrar, Straus & Giroux, 2018), 29. And of course Augustine is always seen in the background of such a narrative.

sinner, and, Fukuyama argues, it was Rousseau who "reversed the Christian moral evaluation of the inner human being."[36] The Sermon presumes Luther's identity as one who stands before God in need of forgiveness, and is therefore charged to act with God's forgiveness toward others. The "blessed" of the Beatitudes are not those recognized and affirmed in the eyes of others, but in God's vision. The inner identity assumed in the Sermon is fundamentally that of the forgiven sinner, the identity that ultimately grounds notions of meekness, humility, and mourning that are not simply self-abnegating.

The second key point is getting visibility right. Here the springboard text is the salt and light metaphors, though it is important to stress in a culture of individualism that the Greek text is properly rendered "y'all are the light of the world"—that the witness function is a *communal* one. Lohfink's term "contrast-society" still serves helpfully to chart a course between a sectarian withdrawal and an anodyne blending in.[37] Yet the dominant visible face of the Christian community should not be one of extravagantly visible pious actions; instead imagine *invisible* piety accompanied by quite *visible* peacemaking, non-lustful, truthful relationships, and the like. True, it's a mistake to assume visible pious actions are inherently insincere. But the emphatic visibility explained in the Sermon is in terms of active seeking of harmony and refusals of the typical dominating strategies of the world, whether through sex, money, speech, anger, or retaliation.

This visibility is of a different kind than the self-defeating third-party element of victimhood culture. We should look at another Matthean discourse, and see that Jesus does not teach "when a brother sins against you, first post it on Twitter; if your brother does not respond, put social media pressure on your brother's institution; if your brother still does not respond, destroy him in every other possible way"! This aspect of victimhood culture has already created a vicious cycle (Trumpism is clearly the manifestation of that). We need to recognize that a community that can really fight against victimization is the one that refuses to victimize the victimizers. That can and should be visible . . . and not the opposite!

The third conclusion is that the ethic of the Sermon requires an account of that lost creedal truth of a final judgment. Here the springboard

---

36. Fukuyama, *Identity*, 30. Taylor also notes that the original sense of the value of inner, individual identity was tied to a relation that inner self has to God ("Politics of Recognition," 28–29).

37. Lohfink, *Jesus and Community*, 122–32, extensively addresses the objections to the term as somehow sectarian or withdrawing from the universal mission of the church.

passage is the famous "do not judge," but with the absolutely essential next part: "lest ye be judged." As I have argued in another recent paper, our strange cultural oscillation between extreme judgmentalism and this edict not to judge (and I wrote it before masks) needs to be confronted with an element of Christianity that has largely disappeared, an account of a final judgment to which all are subject.[38] Our culture is full of people who want to be "in the right," even as we are also repeatedly told to accept everyone as different and unique. Indeed, it's rather amazing that both lessons are so strongly conveyed in our K–12 education culture, without attempts to grapple with the problem created. In the Sermon, the dynamics of non-judgment and mercy are consistently linked to the fact that *all* are subject to judgment. The secret piety is explicitly connected to divine reward, and the economic teaching really does involve taking seriously the idea of a "treasury in heaven."[39] There's a horizon to this whole thing, and while it really does seek peace in the here and now, it recognizes that there is an ultimacy that all will face.

Naming this ultimacy rightly is not easy. Indeed, Richard Hays rightly notes that at the heart of Matthew's Gospel is "a serious tension between rigor and mercy" that must be maintained, rather than collapsed in one direction or the other.[40] From my previous article, I draw two points about this. First, both Robert Jenson and Oliver O'Donovan offer an image of the judgment focused on communal identities—a person is judged in light of acts, and what the judgment reveals is the extent to which a person's identification is with Christ or with "other agencies," as Jenson calls them. Similarly, O'Donovan's account of a future world of rest proceeds through the judgment of whether, in such a world, our actions will find their place in that world or be "made of no account by it."[41] In both cases, we are asked to expose the roots of our actions and purify them in light of the gospel. On either side of these culture wars, we need to ask: Out

---

38. See David Cloutier, "Beyond Judgmentalism and Non-Judgmentalism: A Theological Approach to Public Discourse About Social Sins," *Journal of the Society of Christian Ethics* 39 (2019) 269–85.

39. For the Jewish background of the poor as a treasury in heaven, see Gary Anderson, *Charity: The Place of the Poor in the Biblical Tradition* (New Haven, CT: Yale University Press, 2013).

40. Hays, *Moral Vision of the New Testament*, 101.

41. Cloutier, "Beyond Judgmentalism and Non-Judgmentalism," 277–79, quoting Jenson, *Systematic Theology* (New York: Oxford, 1999), 2:332; and O'Donovan, *Ethics as Theology* (Grand Rapids: Eerdmans, 2017), 3:43.

of what identity does the action proceed? Whose am I, really? Whatever judgment means, it means hostile group identities must be drained out of us in order that we genuinely seek first the kingdom.

The other point is made vividly by Rowan Williams, in his book *Resurrection*. Williams specifically goes after the victim/oppressor dynamic and suggests that Jesus' return in peace to his disciples and to the world is a judgment on judgment. It is not simply taking the side of the victim, but overturning the victim/oppressor relationship in two ways—first, by offering the oppressor the opportunity to recognize that their hope lies precisely in the victim, and second, by promising the possibility of transcending oppressor/oppressed dynamics into a new humanity of other kinds of relationships. Most notably, the pure victim of Christ is a reminder that, in one sense, we are all the oppressor. It is a reminder, as Williams puts it bluntly, that "racism is not evil because its victims are good, it is evil because its victims are human."[42] Jesus' example overturns the possibility of pure victimhood while, at the same time, speaking to oppressors an insistent word that it is their victims who will be their hope.

This entire concern about appropriate judgment is especially important to consider in light of the problem of historically inerasable injustices. I have long recommended an excellent article by an Irish Jesuit Balthasarian, Gerry O'Hanlon, who explains accessibly how a process of both justice and reconciliation needs to work for both perpetrators and victims in a situation like Northern Ireland.[43] O'Hanlon emphasizes the need for truth telling and the need for some sorts of symbols of reparation (as victimhood culture does). Yet he also notes that the process cannot even yield truth telling without the offer of forgiveness from victims to oppressors, and with a willingness by victims to absorb some of the suffering that cannot be undone. He suggests that this is precisely what God did in Christ, suffering on the cross. Christianity can face the challenge of recognizing the reality of the historical truth claim about victimhood while disabling it from perpetuating a cycle of group-on-group struggle.

This judgment is ultimately enacted eschatologically. Yet the judgment rightly spurs us to act in certain ways right now. The Sermon seeks that the dynamics of the eschaton begin to be enacted now, that "thy will be done on earth as it is in heaven." William Mattison's recent treatment

---

42. Rowan Williams, *Resurrection* (Harrisburg, PA: Morehouse, 1994), 17.

43. Gerry O'Hanlon, "Justice and Reconciliation," in *Reconciliation in Religion and Society*, ed. Michael Hurley (Belfast: Institute of Irish Studies, 1994), 48–67.

of the Beatitudes argues rightly that the Beatitudes do not simply mark a kind of eschatological reversal—bad now, but good later—but instead, they invite activity that is intrinsic to their promised "rewards." Yet they do not all do so in the same way. He suggests very helpfully that the last two Beatitudes—the peacemakers and the pure of heart—most fully exhibit activity now that is continuous with the eschatological kingdom.[44] Thus, they may be the most important identities that the church has to bring to the current cultural situation. Peacemaking and purity of heart might be said to be the outward and inward stances by which we can approach the serious issues raised by social movements reverencing victims—genuine, unstinting compassion for those suffering, and at the same time a constant seeking after reconciliation rather than revenge.

Indeed, Christians, like those in the moral culture of victimhood, do believe in a revolution. However, the charter of that revolution for us is the Sermon on the Mount. This means there really is a moral arc to the universe, and it bends toward justice. Our role is to be a more disciplined and better witness to the trajectory of that moral arc, not only in our profession of faith, but most importantly in our actions. Thus, the way the Sermon ends has always been of the greatest importance to me. We are reminded that praising Jesus' fine words, his brilliant initiatives, is not the goal; we must instead build our houses on them.

---

44. William Mattison III, *The Sermon on the Mount and Christian Ethics: A Virtue Perspective* (New York: Cambridge University Press, 2017), 43–44.

4

Is the Sermon on the Mount Economically Realistic?

Brent Waters

WHEN THE EDITOR INVITED me to write on this theme, he offered the title as a tentative suggestion that I could change later. I haven't changed it, but it is important to note that a lot hinges on the word "realistic." A lengthy philological inquiry would severely tax my abilities and your patience as a reader, so I will only briefly indicate what I mean by the word "realistic" and how I will be using it in this chapter.

Something is real when it exists independently in its own right and is not an imaginative construct. England is a real country; Narnia is not. This does not mean that imagination is not important; it is, and it is highly influential. Narnia is more interesting, and perhaps in some circles better known than England. But what is real is not synonymous with what is imagined. Waging war against Nazi Germany and battling Mordor are not the same things. A realistic assessment, then, requires that I must deal with the thing as it is, and not as I might prefer it to be. What is real is not a rhetorical artifact but an object to be described and assessed.

The thing I am dealing with is the economy, by which I mean global markets that match supply and demand for such overlapping interests as goods and services, labor, and capital. The reality of markets is not in dispute. Even the world's largest Communist regime is an avid and adept market player. What is contested is the extent to which governments should regulate or manipulate markets. Consequently, any realistic assessment of the Sermon on the Mount's applicability to the economy must take the reality of markets into account. In making this assessment I am using the following question as a rough guideline: Do some key precepts in the Sermon offer any realistic moral guidance for participating in or regulating global markets?

My answer to the question "Is the Sermon on the Mount economically realistic?" has evolved through four phases: no, yes, maybe, it's complicated. The remainder of this chapter is a tour of how and why my thinking changed.

No

In my initial rereading of the Sermon on the Mount I did not find any items that were of much realistic value, because in some respects it seems hostile to money, commerce, possessions, and the like, the stuff of economics. For instance, we are warned not to accumulate possessions because they will end up being destroyed or stolen (Matt 6:19–21). More ominously, we may be tempted to place our hope and confidence in our treasures or, worse, come to love them. We would then be committing the sin of idolatry, for as Martin Luther warns whatever our hearts cling to is properly our god. We cannot serve both God and Mammon, and we must choose one or the other. Wealth is a grave moral hazard best avoided because most people lack the resolve to resist its allure. Wealthy people are often proud and vain, believing they are superior to those less well off. But they are wrong, even foolish, for it is not the rich but the poor who are blessed by God (5:3).

More generally, the Sermon is indifferent to economics. The marketplace is, at best, a distraction that draws our attention away from what is most important. Our foremost priority should be seeking the righteousness of God's kingdom, and when we faithfully do so what we truly need is provided (Matt 6:33). Consequently, we are enjoined not to worry about what we should eat, drink, or wear (6:31). Our daily bread—a shorthand for what we really need—is given to us by God and not the marketplace (6:11). Our gaze should be directed toward the horizon of our eternal destiny and not the worldly, passing affairs lying in between.

If the Sermon has nothing realistic to say about economics because it is a realm best avoided or ignored, then this chapter would be concluded. It continues, however, because a clear no can't be the right answer. Granted, the contemporary global economy is worldly, filled with sinful temptations and moral hazards. Yet it is also part of God's good creation and therefore a proper object of our love and stewardship. In Luther's words, "We are not made for fleeing human company, but for living in society and sharing good and evil."[1] To treat economics with disdain or indifference because it is worldly is to adopt a gnostic or Manichean stance, but not one that is Christian. Seeking God's kingdom includes attending to the material well-being of its inhabitants.

Yes

Since no is the wrong answer, I assumed that yes must be the right one. The vocabulary of the Sermon suggests this is the case. Like all sermons, what is said presupposes what is not said but is known by the audience to be true. In other words, it goes without saying. For example, if I tell you to wear a warm coat in the winter, I assume you know that your wardrobe is incomplete and there are other items of clothing you also need to wear. Likewise in the Sermon, the teaching concerning possessions should not be understood as total condemnation. Since humans are physical, embodied creatures there are certain needs that must be met and met in an organized manner. Again Luther: "We are not to run away from property, house, home, wife, and children, wandering around the countryside as a burden to other people."[2] Humans living together in a society require an economy to receive their daily bread. The Sermon must therefore have some realistic teaching to offer.

Presumably it does, and there are at least two possible ways for offering this counsel. First, the Sermon's condemnation of possessions and commerce is not as harsh as it appears to be. The Sermon provides spiritual guidance for Christians. Much of its teaching thereby transcends or is not directly pertinent to the secular affairs of the world. Does this mean that Christians are somehow immune from participating in economies that are part of the secular world? No, but they do not do so as Christians, but as human beings constrained by the necessities of their physical and temporal condition.

---

1. Martin Luther, "The Sermon on the Mount," in *Luther's Works* (St. Louis: Concordia, 1956), 21:86.
2. Luther, "Sermon on the Mount," 21:14.

Luther makes this separation explicit by insisting that every human being consists of two persons, one belonging solely to God and the other serving his earthly neighbors.[3] In serving these neighbors, the secular person requires money and possessions, more broadly, markets in which goods and services are produced and exchanged. Accumulating and exchanging possessions cannot be prohibited, otherwise society could not function. People require the wherewithal to maintain their lives and families, and markets are an efficient mechanism for achieving this worthwhile goal. People have a fundamental right to eat, drink, rest, to provide for their material well-being. Consequently, Christians participate in worldly affairs, but as secular persons. Possessions and riches are not inherently evil, but Luther recognizes that the strong temptation of greed must be resisted. He insists that Christ commands us to "live a moderate, sober, and disciplined life,"[4] one in which we obtain and use only the goods and services that we truly need. Practically this entails a detached attitude toward possessions, that we should be happy to lend them, give them away, or let them be taken without complaint. What most concerns Luther is that even Christians in performing secular functions may inadvertently become servants of Mammon by becoming too captivated by the transitory ways of the world and neglecting their eventual destiny. In his words: "It means thinking only about this life, about how to get rich here and how to accumulate and increase our money and property, as though we were going to stay here forever."[5] This insistence on the utilitarian character of economics is realistic counsel.

A second approach rejects the notion that the secular world is of only scant secondary importance and concern. To the contrary, it is the only significant setting for Christian mission. The Sermon on the Mount does not offer implicit, hesitant advice for keeping one's purity of faith while venturing into a hostile earthly domain. Rather, the Sermon is a manual for transforming the world in Christ's name. The new Jerusalem will be built through the faithful efforts of Christ's earthly followers. What the Sermon suggests is that something is terribly wrong with conventional economics, a dire condition requiring radical reform. The Sermon is the template of this reformation. If the moral teachings of Jesus were taken seriously, we would have a different economy, a far better economy. If for instance, we would incorporate the Beatitudes into our daily lives, follow the precepts of

---

3. See Luther, "Sermon on the Mount," 21:66–76.
4. Luther, "Sermon on the Mount," 21:162.
5. Luther, "Sermon on the Mount," 21:193.

the Lord's Prayer, be the salt of the earth, be generous benefactors, go the second mile, and be unattached to possessions, we would have a far more just economy, a socialist economy.

Linking Christian social and moral precepts with socialism has been a profitable cottage industry for nearly the last two centuries. In short, the dominant strand in progressive Protestant ethics, along with supportive Catholic voices, has exhibited a pronounced antipathy to capitalism and warm embrace of socialism because the latter is presumably more compatible with Christian faith and practice. Charles William Stubbs, a late nineteenth-century Anglican cleric, serves as a convenient exemplar. Stubbs argued that a socialist society is possible if we follow Christ's core commands, that such a society embodies the true religion Christ proclaimed. Before this society can be built, however, the social and political ground must first be cleared. The most pressing tasks at hand include redistributing wealth, mitigating the "tyranny of capital," and abolishing the "unfair monopoly of profit."[6] Humans do not own property or wealth but are God's stewards holding them "in trust for the common well-being."[7] Stubbs goes on to offer some basic principles for exercising this stewardship: The "true social order . . . should have for its basis not the accumulation of wealth through self-interest and competition, but human progress and well-being, through self-sacrifice and association." Civil society "exists not for the sake of private property, but private property for the sake of society." There is a religious duty of justice to ensure that common wants are met, and wealth should enable the rich "to do unpaid work for society."[8] Stubbs believes that he is not proffering vague, utopian sentiments, but offering a realistic proposal: "We might be all safely Socialists to-morrow, if we were only really Christians to-day."[9]

Answering yes to the realistic applicability of the Sermon on the Mount requires exercising one of two possible options (and only one, for they are mutually exclusive). On the one hand, economics is a necessity consigned, rightly, to the secular world. The Sermon provides guidance on how best to be a Christian while meeting material needs and wants, a stance of casual indifference regarding the ways of the world to resist the temptations

---

6. Charles William Stubbs, *Christ and Economics in the Light of the Sermon on the Mount* (London: Isbister, 1894), 92.

7. Stubbs, *Christ and Economics*, 116.

8. Stubbs, *Christ and Economics*, 116–17.

9. Stubbs, *Christ and Economics*, 114.

of Mammon. In a crude sense the Sermon is a handbook for retaining a dovelike innocence while being a wise serpent in the marketplace. Let's call this the advice option. On the other hand, ordering economic activity in accordance with the gospel is a chief element in building the kingdom of God on earth. The Sermon is an agenda for Christian action designed not simply to resist Mammon but to vanquish him. In a rough sense, the Sermon is an architectural digest for constructing the new Jerusalem. Let's call this the blueprint option. I find neither option to be entirely satisfactory, which forces me to step back, reassess, and change my answer regarding the realistic applicability of the Sermon on the mount to maybe.

Maybe

My principal objection to the advice option is its dualism. The layers of human life are divided in half, for instance, sacred and secular, spiritual and physical, soul and body. These divisions correspond roughly with the command to love God and neighbor, but they are effectively presented as two separate loves. One is an intangible exercise virtually devoid of any sensual perception, while the other is fixed exclusively on that which is tangible and accessible to the senses. There are no scriptural or theological warrants, however, for this divide. Creation and its creatures do not somehow straddle unrelated loves. Rather, there is a singular love manifested in pluriform ways. The creator is not absent from the creation; the world is not godless. At a minimum, sacramentality reveals that secular space and physical objects can be fitting hosts for the sacred and spiritual. People do not live in a conflict between body and soul but are embodied souls and ensouled bodies.[10]

If the Sermon on the Mount is to provide realistic advice, then it must resist these artificial bifurcations, a resistance justified by the incarnation in which God was pleased to become a human creature and dwell among us. Consequently, attending to the material well-being of people is not a peripheral concern but a central practice in loving one's neighbors. We demonstrate neighbor love, in part, by providing neighbors with the goods and services they need. And to love our neighbors by attending to their material needs is to also exhibit love for the incarnate God.

---

10. See Paul Ramsey, *The Patient as Person: Explorations in Medical Ethics* (New Haven, CT: Yale University Press, 1970), xiii.

The Sermon, and Scripture more broadly, recognize this motivation and aim of love pervading the commonplace items and relationships of everyday life. Luther comments, "If you are a manual laborer, you find that the Bible has been put into your workshop, into your hand, into your heart."[11] Settling for shoddy work, for example, is mistreating one's neighbor. In replying to the question "What . . . does 'daily bread' mean?" Luther offers this summary: "Everything included in the necessities and nourishment of our bodies, such as food, drink, clothing, shoes, house, farm, fields, livestock, money, property, and upright spouses, upright children, upright members of the household, upright and faithful rulers, good government, good weather, peace, health, decency, honor, good friends, faithful neighbors and the like."[12] It is in the mundane act of receiving our daily bread that we catch a glimmer of loving God and neighbor.

My primary objection to the blueprint option is that it consists of an attractive idea that almost never works in the real world. There is a long, and some would add venerable, history of Christian socialism. It presents an appealing picture of humans living and working together peacefully, balancing labor and leisure, and enjoying a just distribution of wealth. It is a community where people help and care for one another; solidarity of purpose has replaced the predatory individualism of the market economy. The Sermon on the Mount is the guiding document for constructing this new Jerusalem.

There is no reason to deny the appeal of this envisioned future, for it has consistently attracted devoted followers. There is also no reason to deny its long, and some would add sordid, history of failure. This history begins in the New Testament. The Acts of the Apostles records that Christians residing in Jerusalem "were of one heart and mind" holding "everything in common" (4:32). They soon became a bitterly divided and destitute church. Christian history is littered with the rise and fall of utopian communities that come and go with alarming frequency. The exceptions are some monastic, Anabaptist, and sectarian communities. Yet ironically, those that have survived for an extended period of time have done so by adapting to the worldly economies that they are trying to escape. Monasteries have often started and overseen successful commercial ventures, the Amish operate well-managed farms and are shrewd

---

11. Luther, "Sermon on the Mount," 21:137.

12. As quoted in Mark D. Tranvik, *Martin Luther and the Called Life* (Minneapolis: Fortress, 2016), 149.

businessmen, at their peak the Shakers were known for their furniture that fetched a high price, and the Amana commune simply morphed into a corporation. But these are rare exceptions.

How may we account for this history of failed implementation? It may be that the Sermon on the Mount was never meant to be a blueprint. Jesus' teachings are unrealistic ideals that cannot and will not be implemented until God's kingdom is established in Christ's return. Attempts at implementing the Sermon before the parousia are doomed to fail because they are impractical. But this evades the real issue at stake. The problem is not that the economy of the Sermon is unrealistic, but that humans refuse to change their values and behavior in line with its basic socialistic precepts. With a change of heart an economy of sharing will replace that of competition. We should not abandon hope but wait for the Spirit to prompt an awakening in which our disordered desires are realigned with God's will, giving us in turn the wisdom and courage to build the kingdom in God's name. Despite a history of failed attempts, all that is needed is one, final success.

To summarize, the Sermon on the Mount is economically realistic if it is viewed as offering practical advice for serving our neighbors as best we can in a fallen and imperfect world. With the aid of Christ's grace, we conduct ourselves in an honest and forthright manner in the rough-and-tumble of the marketplace. We must deal with the world as it is. In contrast, the gospel is urging us to change the world into what it should be. The Sermon provides the model we ought to be constructing after we allow the Spirit to convert our values and desires accordingly. So, which is it? Advice or a blueprint? This leads me to my final answer: it's complicated.

It's Complicated

One complication is the vast gulf separating the Sermon on the Mount from our present circumstances. The economy of Jesus' day is simply unlike ours.[13] The teachings reproving wealth and property, for instance, were made in the context of an economy based predominantly on the natural fecundity of the earth. Wealth was derived from such things as precious metals, timber, and most importantly food. When wealth is

---

13. The remainder of this paragraph and the following one are taken, with minor revisions, from Brent Waters, *Just Capitalism: A Christian Ethic of Economic Globalization* (Louisville: Westminster John Knox, 2016), 34–35.

based on the land the resulting economy is a zero-sum game because land is limited—the easiest way to increase one's wealth is to acquire someone else's property. This was accomplished by conquest or seizing land as payment of debt or taxes. The criticisms of wealth exposed the injustice of a system in which the wealthy obtained their riches by seizing the property of others. Redistributing wealth and prohibiting usury were ways of protecting the weaker players in a zero-sum economy, and selling one's possessions was also a way of decreasing one's vulnerability since the rich cannot seize what the poor do not possess.

The contemporary global economy, however, is not a zero-sum game, for wealth is created primarily by producing and consuming goods and services through trade and commercial transactions. Productivity is not entirely a tangible thing derived from land and is therefore not as limited; for instance, producing and purchasing digitized information. Increased productivity is the principal way of increasing wealth. The wealthy do not become rich because they somehow seize productivity from someone else, but in creating greater opportunities for economic exchange. Through increased productivity, commerce, and employment, both rich and poor ideally benefit even though an expanding income gap often results. Moreover, productivity and the consumption of goods and services are predicated upon available capital, finance, labor, and credit. To simply apply the seemingly "clear" teachings of redistributing wealth, prohibiting interest-bearing loans, and liberating oneself from possessions would probably harm rather than help the poor, particularly in lesser-developed countries.

The Sermon's practical advice does not translate easily or smoothly from one context to the other. For example, the counsel to refrain from worrying about the future—what we will eat, drink, and wear—is well taken, because there was literally little or nothing the poor comprising 80–90 percent of the population could do to provide for themselves in the future. Their trust should be placed in God, who would provide what they needed through the love of family, benevolence of friends, or charity of strangers. Hence the moral obligation for almsgiving found in the New Testament and patristic teaching. That is a reality far removed from widespread access to social security, pensions, and 401ks enjoyed by a burgeoning global middle class. Poverty remains a stubborn problem in both developed and developing economies, but it is not the dominant social reality as was the case in the Sermon's social setting. If God provides what is needed, does this preclude saving for the future when one has the wherewithal to do so? Or is financial planning mistrusting God's providential care?

If the Sermon is a blueprint, it is also difficult to see how it transfers from an ancient to a late modern setting. The Sermon propounds many sound moral precepts and aphorisms. Who could quarrel with telling the truth, going the second mile, philanthropy, or peacemaking? But there are scant details concerning their implementation on a large scale in our present circumstances. For instance, what kind of policies help or hinder the poor and meek in respect to taxes, fiscal policies, and market regulations? If the Sermon is a blueprint, it requires a lot of updating. It's a bit like trying to build a skyscraper by starting with an old sketch of a hut. But perhaps this kind of arduous work is what Christ is calling his followers of every age to undertake. The call for social justice in our own day is but another step in this process of updating.

This task of reconciling contrasting contexts is challenging, even daunting, but not insurmountable. Preachers and theologians, after all, regularly translate the old into the new. Yet even if this translation is performed efficiently and faithfully, it will not determine definitively whether the Sermon is advice or a blueprint. Why? Because substantial disagreements will remain regarding how economic ordering should be evaluated, and these conflicting evaluations are derived from differing understandings of core Christian convictions. I'll use three examples to illustrate these differences.

First, how is neighbor love best exhibited within an economic order? Economics teaches us that interacting with neighbors is unavoidable and necessary. A cursory understanding of economics quickly dispels the fiction of autonomy. We cannot secure our daily bread by going it alone; we need each other. Customers need merchants, and merchants need customers; borrowers need bankers, and bankers need borrowers; employees need employers, and employers need employees, etc. There is no dispute that every day we encounter countless neighbors in both physical marketplaces and virtual market spaces, the same neighbors we are commanded to love. Here Christians disagree over what this love requires.

If, for instance, the Sermon on the Mount is a catalog of practical advice, then competitive global markets are the best venues for loving our neighbors, especially our poor ones. At the macro level the prominence of global markets has benefited the poor. In the last two decades nearly a billion people have been lifted out of dire poverty, almost exclusively through increased participation in expanding global markets. Loving our neighbors means ensuring they learn the skills and have access to markets where they may successfully compete. But there is a downside to this scenario. When markets are working correctly, they disrupt by promoting a process that Joseph Schumpeter calls "creative destruction."[14] Innovative products or better ways of doing business are creative but also destroy competitors in the process. Does anyone remember RCA, Blockbuster, the Sears catalog, or Polaroid cameras? Although disruption benefits most consumers over time, many individuals suffer unemployment or underemployment for short or extended periods of time. In these instances, neighbor love requires some kind of safety net so that new, more applicable, and competitive skills can be learned. The realistic advice of the Sermon is to make sure you can earn your daily bread.

In contrast, if the Sermon on the Mount is a blueprint, then we should aspire to protect our neighbors from the destructive forces of global markets. It is, after all, the humble, and not fierce, competitors who will inherit the earth. Neighbor love requires an economy that rewards generosity, resists materialism, promotes solidarity, and most importantly eliminates the anxiety of turbulent markets. We should not be forced to worry about obtaining our daily bread. As noted earlier, proponents insist this blueprint is socialist rather than capitalist, and if history is any guide, this practical expression of neighbor love entails highly regulated markets to ensure steady production and employment, and high taxation to pay for social services and redistribution of wealth. There is steady leveling in which the gap separating rich and poor continually shrinks. Again, if history is a reliable guide, GDP will decline, as too the quantity and quality of available goods. But this is a reasonable price to pay to ensure that the basic needs of every neighbor are met. A corrupting consumerism is replaced with time to share more simple pleasures with friends and family. The Sermon provides the basic principles for promoting the love of God and neighbor while resisting Mammon's enchantments.

Second, the Sermon on the Mount may be understood with differing eschatologies in mind. If one believes that the end comes in a manner beyond our control, then the Sermon is advice for living in the meantime. We must do what is required to sustain our material well-being, but this is not our ultimate aim. Hence, the warning against accumulating riches, for

---

14. See Joseph A. Schumpeter, *Capitalism, Socialism and Democracy* (New York: Harper Perennial, 2008), ch. 7; see also Waters, *Just Capitalism*, ch. 3.

they can only disappoint and distract our attention away from the more important task of caring for our souls. In general, the Sermon may be understood as illuminating faithful and patient waiting, waiting, that is, in a twofold sense. We wait, when in the fullness of time, the poor, meek, merciful, and pure in heart are fully blessed by God. In this time between the times, we also wait on one another, serving each other and meeting our various needs. And a prominent place for performing this waiting is the marketplace. This waiting presupposes that our destiny is entirely God's initiative, coming unexpectedly as a thief in the night.

Reading the Sermon on the Mount as a blueprint, however, presupposes a very different eschatology. We must take the initiative in building God's kingdom in the here and now. The poor, meek, merciful, and pure in heart will be blessed when we build a just economic order. It is not patient waiting that should command our attention, but urgent, faithful work as demanded by the dictates of our Lord's Sermon. The Sermon, in general, may be understood as a summons to be agents exercising God's will on earth.

The respective strengths and weaknesses of these eschatologies mirror each other. The chief strength of waiting is that it is cautious. Humans should be cautious since as fallible, fallen, and sinful creatures they have a strong proclivity toward screwing things up, a tendency reflected in the economic principle of unintended consequences. In other words, we are adept at desiring good things badly. For example, policies intending to help workers may end up destroying their jobs. Consequently, our actions should be restrained so we at least limit the damage that might be done. The weakness is that such so-called prudence may be an excuse for doing nothing, effectively maintaining the status quo in which the few benefits at the expense of the many. It is avarice disguised as waiting.

Those following the Sermon's blueprint, however, do not suffer from hesitancy. Bold, decisive action must be taken immediately to establish justice, relieving the poor from their plight. To respond to the Lord's Sermon is to bear the heavy burden to do no less than change the course of history. Yet even the most ardent followers remain sinners, and faith morphs into pride, or worse. History is littered with the wreckage of sweeping economic and political reforms effectively becoming exercises in tyranny, or worse. The blueprint of the Sermon becomes a map for the road to serfdom.

Third, how we understand the Sermon on the Mount differs if we assume that the Christian life is one of pilgrimage or homesteading. In the

City of God, St. Augustine is clear that Christians are pilgrims. As Christians we are citizens of the heavenly city but presently reside in the earthly city. We are never entirely at home in this world because we ultimately do not belong here; our destination is the heavenly city where we will enjoy eternal fellowship with the triune God. Christians are always a bit restless and on the move, awaiting, as patiently as they can, their homecoming. This does not mean, however, that they despise the world and its inhabitants. To the contrary, the world remains God's good creation, and its human inhabitants bear the image and likeness of their creator. Pilgrims are still called to love God's handiwork and serve their neighbors. And it doesn't matter where one is to express this love and perform this service. Since pilgrims do not belong anywhere in the world it doesn't matter where they are to be faithful followers of Jesus Christ. Consequently, the fluidity and uncertainty of markets, even their creative destruction, are not problems to be solved. As pilgrims, Christians need to be a mobile and adaptable people. The Sermon, then, serves as a reminder in our earthly pilgrimage to stay focused on the destination, but not to be oblivious to the journey. Serve your neighbors, tell the truth, go the second mile, pray, fast, and most importantly do not be anxious about the future because your hope is in God.

In contrast, homesteaders see the world and their life in it much differently. Stability, not disruption, is the lynchpin of a good life. People need to settle down rather than wander about, build a life for themselves and others in a particular place. Markets, then, need to be regulated and controlled so they don't threaten a settled way of life, don't destroy communities that have provided a place of belonging from one generation to another. The Sermon provides guidance for establishing and sustaining this stability. Wealth is to be shared so no one goes without. We are to be reconciled with one another so jealousy and resentment do not smolder. Our works will be as good fruit stemming from pure hearts, and in being the salt of the earth and light to the nations, Christians will build a city on a hill as a witness to God's rule, a stable economic order based on envisioning and living out a righteous kingdom.

Again, the principal strength of each of these understandings is the weakness of the other. A life of pilgrimage recognizes that Christianity is life in the Spirit. The Spirit does not domesticate but blows where it will. God is not calling us to lives of predictable safety, but the adventure of traversing unknown lands. But sometimes pilgrims become so fixed on the destination that they forget the importance of the journey. They fail to see or serve the neighbors they encounter along the way and fail to acknowledge that pilgrims must stop and belong somewhere, at least for a while. Homesteaders recognize the importance of being in place. Truly loving the world and serving one's neighbors requires the stability of being still and interacting with familiar faces day in and day out. But in preferring the familiar, the homesteader may fail to heed the calling of the Spirit. Change itself becomes an enemy, at times effectively justifying unjust practices and relationships. When stability becomes an idol, then a call to pack up and enter a new land becomes suspect, even treasonous.

I have now reached that awkward point in this chapter that I wish I could ignore, for you, dear reader, may be asking, So which is it? Is the Sermon on the Mount advice, or is it a blueprint? A safe option would be to reject both options, but explaining why would require at least another chapter, and none of us, including my editors, wants that. Or I could say in effect that my job was to provide some options, and you are now on your own to choose one. But it doesn't seem right for the author to effectively abandon the reader after coming this far. So, I will offer an answer and briefly explain why.

If the Sermon on the Mount is economically realistic, then it should be understood as advice rather than a blueprint. The best way to love our global neighbors is equipping them to participate and compete in markets that enable them to attend to their material well-being in ways that they choose. The freedom to encounter and disrupt markets is better than trying to prevent it through centralized planning and regulation. The instability of markets is preferable to the tyranny of experts imposing inflexible plans that do not work because they stifle initiative. Bakeries catering to customers in free markets are best equipped for providing adequate supplies of daily bread. Is this risky? Yes, and there is nothing in the Sermon implying we should be risk averse. Indeed, love—including the love of neighbor—is meaningless in the absence of risk, for any activity devoid of possible failure is not worth pursuing in the first place. It is not coincidental that the most protective economic and political orders are also the most loveless.

The future is something we wait for rather than manufacture. In Jesus' resurrection and promised return, the future has already occurred, and we wait to be embraced by it. This is why the Sermon enjoins us not to worry. This does not mean that in waiting we do nothing, for we also wait upon our neighbors, especially those in greatest need. And we encounter most of our neighbors in the marketplace. Waiting is not an excuse for inactivity but serves as a warning against any conceit that we are clever enough to build God's kingdom on our own terms. Rather, it is through such ordinary activities as work and commerce that we prepare ourselves to receive this kingdom as a gift. Perceiving the future as a gift we receive or an artifact we fabricate goes a long way in shaping how we live in the present, including our lives as producers and consumers. The Sermon offers practical advice for faithful waiting, for living faithfully in this time between the times.

Finally, Christians are pilgrims rather than homesteaders. Christianity has never been a territorial religion. The church exists whenever and wherever two or three are gathered in Christ's name. The old hymn is right, this world is not our home, we are just passing through. But passing through does not mean ignoring or despising the world. This world and its inhabitants are God's good creation that we are commanded to love, and to love as a material reality, teeming with creaturely needs demanding to be met. Even as pilgrims on the move we know the importance of exchange and trade that puts bread on the table, a roof over one's head, and shelter for resting. And the economy used to satisfy these needs functions best in an environment of mutual trust. This is why much of the Sermon is devoted to offering advice on being honest and forthright. As pilgrims we are free to love and wait upon our neighbors wherever in the world we encounter them, including global markets.

Martin Luther once said, "There are three things . . . which every good preacher should do: First, he takes his place; second, he opens his mouth and says something; third, he knows when to stop."[15] What is true for a preacher is also true for an author, so I will stop by asking one last time: Is the Sermon on the Mount economically realistic? No . . . yes . . . maybe . . . it's complicated, very complicated.

---

15. Luther, "Sermon on the Mount," 21:7.

5

Preaching the Sermon on the Mount

Sarah Hinlicky Wilson

My topic is "Preaching the Sermon on the Mount," so I will begin by, quite literally, preaching the Sermon on the Mount.[1]

> Seeing the crowds
> Jesus ascended the mountain.
> When he sat down,
> his disciples approached him.
> And opening his mouth
> he taught them,
> saying:
>
> Blessed: the forlorn and forsaken
>   the hurting and heartsick
>   the humane and restrained
>   the famished and parched
>   for righteousness.
>
> Theirs: the kingdom of heaven
>   the solace and succor

---

[1]. This paper began as a lecture, and its oral quality has been only slightly edited. Readers might wish to read the first half of it aloud.

The Sermon on the Mount

	the birthright and reign the banquet and feast.
Blessed:	the clement and kindly the wholesome and spotless the steady and peaceful the tarnished and smeared for righteousness.
Theirs:	the kindness and clemency the perceiving and seeing the adoption and kinship the kingdom of heaven.
Blessed:	you.
Blessed:	when they besmirch you
Blessed:	when they browbeat you
Blessed:	when they accuse you due to your alliance
with:	me.

In that day,
hurray!
Rewards
for the reviled
abide in heaven.
For so they pursued
the prophets before you.

You are the salt of the earth.
But if the salt turns stupid,
how will it get resalted?
The salutary thing
is to fling
it out.

You are the light of the world.
Secret cities don't sit
    on mountaintops.
Lighted lamps don't lurk
    under measuring cups.
So
light your lamp.
Hang it high.
Those you illumine
will give glory to God in heaven.

Don't imagine that
I came
to unravel
the law and the prophets.
I came
not to unravel
but to knit back together.

I promise you:
Until heaven and earth perish
neither the dot of an i
nor the stroke of a serif
will perish from the law
until all the things that are going to happen
happen.

So
whoever frays the edge of
the least little commandment
and urges folks to do the same
will be sheared off the kingdom of heaven.

But
whoever stitches them up
and urges folks to do the same
will be woven into the kingdom of heaven.

The Sermon on the Mount

Unless you are of uncut cloth
seamless
smooth
and whole
you will not grace
the banquet tables of heaven.

You've heard how
the first folks were told:
Don't kill.
Whoever kills is gonna get it.

But I promise you:
Anyone who snarls
at her nearest and dearest
is gonna get it.
Anyone who growls
at his next of kin,
"You bastard,"
is gonna get it in court.
Anyone who sneers,
"You moron,"
is gonna get it in hell.

So
if you're writing a check for charity
or chanting along in church
and remember how a relative
has cause to be cross at you—
Stop everything.
Get out of there.
Work things out.
Then your worship will be worthwhile.

Make nice with the opposition
and do it quick
en route
or else

they'll give you to the judge,
and the judge to the guard,
and the guard to the jail.
I promise you:
You won't escape
till you pay back
every
last
penny.

You've heard how they were told:
Don't mess around with another man's wife.
But what I say is,
everyone who looks at a woman
(you know how I mean)
already adulterates her in his heart.

So if your right eye wrongs her,
gouge it out and get rid of it.
Better one part perishes
than the whole in hell.
And if your right hand wrongs her,
hack it off and hurl it away.
Better one part perishes
than the whole in hell.

And they were told:
Whoever divorces his wife,
do it nice and legal.
But what I say is,
everyone who divorces his wife
(except on account of her messing around
with another woman's husband)
adulterates her
and whoever marries a divorced woman
adulterates himself.

The Sermon on the Mount

Again, you're aware
they were told: Beware!
Grant God what you swear
in your prayer.
But I declare:
Do not swear!
Not by heaven. It is God's chair.
Not by earth. His feet rest there.
Do not swear by anywhere.
No, not even by your hair.
More than "yes" or "no" is to err
beyond repair.

Eye for eye.
Tooth for tooth.
Fair is fair.
But what I say is,
don't defy your foe.
Whoever gives you a right hook,
offer him an uppercut.
Whoever sues for your overcoat,
hand him also your undershirt.
Whoever makes you walk one mile,
lead him on for two.

They ask?
You give.
They borrow?
You lend.

The rules plainly state:
Friends are to love;
Enemies, to hate.
Your Father above
says, as I say, to you:
Enemies are to love
And those who harm you.
Your Father above

Sends down the rain
On all, out of love,
Just and unjust the same,
And his sun up above.
His sons act likewise.
For what if you love
Only those, in your eyes,
Who are good? Far above
Basic pay will you get?
It's your brothers you love.
Does this goodwill set
You a notch up above?
Love only for these
Is a small kind of love.
Love your enemies,
Like your Father above.

So
be
perfect,
like
your
Father
in
heaven
is
perfect.

See to it that
your righteousness
is not seen.
Recognized righteousness
goes unrewarded.

So
when you give alms
don't give an almighty *BLAST*
like the hypocrites do

in the alleys and avenues
to be praised by people.
I guarantee you,
they've gotten everything they're gonna get.
But as for you,
when you're giving alms,
it's sinister to see
what your own self is doing.
Keep it covered.
And your Father,
hidden in heaven,
will balance the books.

And
when you pray
don't be like the hypocrites
who have to assemble
in the alleys and avenues
so others observe them.
I guarantee you,
they've gotten everything they're gonna get.
But as for you,
when you pray,
go into your closet and close it.
Keep it covered.
And your Father,
hidden in heaven,
will pay attention
to your petition.

And when you pray
don't *b-b-b-blather* like the *b-b-b-barbarians*
who believe their logorrhea
makes their listeners listen.
Don't be like them.
Your Father
knows what you need
before you even ask.

Here's how you should pray.
Our Father
in heaven
holy—be your name
here—come your kingdom
heaven—do on earth
tomorrow's bread
bestow today
when we release
our debtors,
release us
from our debts
spare us the trial
spare us the test
save us from evil
and all of the rest!

Forgive others,
and your Father will forgive you.
Refrain from forgiving others,
and your Father will refrain from forgiving you.

And when you fast
don't do like
the frowny faces do
so folks know they're fasting.
I guarantee you,
they've gotten everything they're gonna get.
But when you fast
wash up,
stand up,
chin up,
so no one knows.
Keep it covered.
And your Father,
hidden in heaven,
will repay your pangs.

The Sermon on the Mount

Many treasure treasure
    on earth where
moths munch on it
decay devours it
robbers ransack it.
If you treasure treasure
    in heaven where
moths are missing
decay is denied
robbers are refused,
you will cherish
what won't perish.

The lamp of your life is your eye.
So
if your eye is laser-focused
your whole being is bright.
But
if your eye is evil
your whole being is dark.
So
if the light in you
is darkness—
        how great
                the darkness

You can't obey two lords
at the same time.
You'll hate the one
and love the other
or
you'll support the one
and undermine the other.
You can't obey both
God and Gold.

Which is why I say:
Don't pull yourself apart with
"What'll I eat?" or "What'll I wear?"

Isn't your soul greater than its sustenance
and your figure than its finery?
Sparrows don't sow.
Robins don't reap.
Blackbirds don't build barns.
Yet your Father in heaven
harbors the birds of heaven
under his wings.
You goose!
Aren't you worth more than a warbler?

Does pulling yourself apart
add height to your heels?
And concerning clothing,
why pull yourself apart?
Learn from the lilies,
which without spinning or sewing grow.
What I'm saying is,
even Solomon in all his fancy finery
couldn't compare to a simple speedwell
or a plain old pink.
So if God decks out
the dandelions and daffodils
that are blooming today
and mown down tomorrow,
won't he do more for you?
Such feeble faith!

So
don't pull yourself apart with
"What'll we eat?" or
"What'll we drink?" or
"What'll we wear?"
The heathen are always on the hunt for these things,
as if your Father in heaven
didn't already know
you need them.

The Sermon on the Mount

First
scope out your Father's kingdom
and survey his righteousness.
Then
all these things
will be annexed to your acreage.

So
don't pull yourself apart
over tomorrow.
Tomorrow can pull itself apart
just fine on its own.
Today's troubles
are more than enough.

Don't damn
so you won't be damned.
For what you dam up
will be denied you, too,
and the meter you mete out
will be meted out to you.

Do you see a twig in your brother's eye? Yes
Have you checked your own eye? No
Check it
Is there a beam in your eye? No
Check again
Is there a beam in your eye? Yes
Remove it
Is the beam still in your eye? Yes
Try again
Is the beam still in your eye? No
Is the twig still in your brother's eye? Yes
Remove it

Don't give the holy
to the hounds,
nor toss your pearls

to the pigs,
lest they trample them,
and turn,
and tackle you!

Ask and you'll receive.
Seek and you'll find.
Knock and you'll be welcomed in.
Everyone who asks receives.
Everyone who seeks finds.
Everyone who knocks is welcomed in.
However evil, will any of you,
if your child asks for bread,
hand over a stone?
However wicked, will any of you,
if your child asks for fish,
hand over a snake?
If you can be good to yours,
how much more will your
Father in heaven
be good to you
if you
        ask
              seek
                      knock!

So
all the things
you wish people
would do for you,
you
do first
for them.
This
is the law and the prophets.

Head for the strait gate,
for broad is the boulevard

and wide is the way
that leads to death.
    Hordes hasten
    to destruction.
But strait is the gate
and wearisome the way
that leads to life.
    Some seek.
    Few find.

Look out for pseudoprophets:
working through the countryside,
sneaking up alongside,
sheep on the outside,
wolves on the inside,
greedy at your graveside.

From their fruits you will recognize them.
For are grapes (*Vitis vinifera*)
gathered from an acanthus (*Acanthus syriacus*)
or figs (*Ficus carica*)
from a puncture vine (*Tribulus terrestris*)?
Good tree $\Rightarrow$ fair fruit.
Rotten tree $\Rightarrow$ evil fruit.
Good tree $\not\Rightarrow$ evil fruit.
Rotten tree $\not\Rightarrow$ fair fruit.
$\therefore$ Rotten tree $\Rightarrow$ fire.
Yes, from their fruits you will recognize them.

Not all who say
Lord! Lord!
enter the kingdom.
But you workers-of-the-will of my Father:
come in.
Many will say
Lord! Lord!
open the kingdom!
Did we not speak out—

    all in your name?
Did we not cast out—
    all in your name?
Did we not act out—
    all in your name?
Then I will say
Never! Ever!
enter the kingdom.
You laborers-of-lawlessness:
depart.

So
everyone who hears these words of mine
and does them
will be like a sage
who built a house on a rock.
And the rain fell
and the rivers came
and the winds blew.
And they struck that house.
And the house did not fall,
for it was built on a rock.

And
everyone who hears these words of mine
and does not do them
will be like a fool
who built a house on the sand.
And the rain fell
and the rivers came
and the winds blew.
And they struck that house.
And it fell.
And great
        was the fall
                of that house.

The Sermon on the Mount

And when it happened that
Jesus finished all these words,
the crowds were
dumbfounded
by his teaching;
for he was teaching
like the one who had
authored all these things,
and not like one of their experts.

The Sermon on the Mount is something that's always just kind of been there—one of those handy points of reference so ubiquitous as to be invisible. As with so many other theological matters in my life, it was forced to the center of my attention by . . . my dad, Paul Hinlicky. He wanted to wrap up our first year of podcasting, in late 2019, with an episode on the topic,[2] and in what I admit now was purely an act of filial piety, I agreed. I was not otherwise interested.

Well, as usual, Dad—and the entire Christian tradition—was right: the Sermon is of course worthy of devout attention. But I was convicted of this *not* by reading the Sermon on the Mount itself, but by reading Luther's commentary thereon, which should, if nothing else, confirm everyone's worst suspicions about Protestants and their so-called *sola Scriptura*.[3] What happened is that, contrary to my expectations, the Reformer did not dismiss the commandments in the Sermon with theological sleight-of-hand on the grounds that we poor miserable sinners couldn't possibly keep them but that's okay because God loves us anyway and let us sin all the more that grace may abound! No, if anything, Luther rails endlessly against those who would let one single Christian off the hook of obeying every last jot and tittle that Jesus commands. Well, if Luther could still surprise this overconfident Lutheran, then it stood to reason that the Lord Christ could also still surprise this anemic Christian.

---

2. That episode can be found at Sarah Hinlicky Wilson and Paul Hinlicky, "The Sermon on the Mount," *Queen of the Sciences*, Oct. 22, 2019; https://www.queenofthesciences.com/e/the-sermon-on-the-mount-1570719979/. A follow-up episode discussing my poetic paraphrase can be found at Sarah Hinlicky Wilson and Paul Hinlicky, "2020 Bonus Episode 5: Sarah's 'Sermon on the Mount,'" *Queen of the Sciences*, Sept. 1, 2020; https://www.queenofthesciences.com/e/2020-bonus-episode-5-sarahs-sermon-on-the-mount/.

3. Martin Luther, "The Sermon on the Mount," in *Luther's Works*, vol. 21, ed. and trans. Jaroslav Pelikan (St. Louis: Concordia, 1956).

What I did find in the process of recording the aforementioned podcast episode, however, was that the Sermon was just too familiar as such to reach me. As I summarized its contents to the microphone, I barely held back from concluding, "It's just one *cliché* after another!," managing to edit myself on the spot to "It's just one *aphorism* after another" instead. Apparently, in my brain, "aphorism" is the politically correct version of "cliché." Poor Sermon on the Mount: victim of its own success.

Now, some of this is down to the text of the Sermon as we have it. The Gospel of Mark is famously accused of being "pearls on a string," and pearls that have been thrown to the pigs at that, but I think the charge is better leveled at the Sermon on the Mount. It's clear enough even to the greatest skeptic of historical-critical method that Jesus did not preach exactly these words in exactly this order. They were linked together somewhere along the way, perhaps by the mysterious Q, centuries before he found a better line of work designing high-tech toys for James Bond. Which means that interpreters are driven to the unpleasant choice between, on the one hand, trying to discern exactly *what* string it is that all these pearls are strung on, such that the pearls get subordinated to the string, or, on the other hand, taking the whole thing apart, pearl by pearl, to get a better look at each one, but jettisoning the real or imagined unity that makes them collectively into one magnificent necklace.

From a scholarly angle, both approaches have their virtues, but from a preacher's perspective, neither is particularly satisfying. In any event, my task was to do the meta-analysis of talking about preaching on the preaching, sermonizing on the Sermon, which explodes multidimensionally outward from the already significant exegetical problems to those of actually communicating some of this pearl necklace's luster to a specific congregation.

So, I went in two directions to accomplish this task, which I'll recount one at a time.

The first was simply to figure out how to speak the Sermon's own words with a fighting chance of them being heard—by me, if no one else. Even if the average congregant is not as immersed in Scripture as the average preacher, chances are good their ears will perk up at the familiar stuff, so reassuringly familiar as to vanish again, while the unfamiliar stuff will float by unnoticed. How to *hear* the Sermon, and how to *speak* the Sermon before preaching on it? Even if Jesus did not deliver the Sermon in precisely the way it's come down to us, the evangelist Matthew still presents it as a sermon, the kind of thing that a preacher *could* deliver. It needed to be heard *as* a sermon before I could cast my own sermonic cloak over it.

My koine Greek having survived the ravages of time better than my Hebrew, I decided to try translating it on my own. I found some nice Easter eggs along the way. The last word of "blessed are those who mourn, for they shall be *comforted*" could be translated instead: "for they shall be *paracleted*." I was so delighted to find the Holy Spirit alighting on the Beatitudes in this cryptic fashion. Speaking of which, I also liked it that all the references to hiddenness in the admonitions on almsgiving, praying, and fasting derive from the same Greek root as "cryptic." Encrypting our religious acts has a nice contemporary resonance about it; God can track users on the blockchain while they remain anonymous to everyone else. And I was more charmed than I probably should have been by the three strategic appearances of the word "moron," a direct borrowing from Greek into English. Unsalty salt is actually "made moron"; the insult that will earn you Gehenna is "you moron"; and yet the foolish man who builds on sand is, according to Jesus' own words, a moron.[4] But then again, Jesus knew he was headed for Gehenna anyway, so maybe he was less nervous about leveling that particular accusation.

Still, making the most of Greek loanwords in English is a limited game and one for dilettantish scholars rather than preachers, so that strategy quickly ran aground. Oddly enough, I ended up getting my decisive inspiration for doing a complete poetic paraphrase from a translation of the Tao Te Ching by sci-fi/fantasy author Ursula K. Le Guin, one of my favorite authors to argue with.[5] Literal translations of the Tao Te Ching abound, but unless you are already privy to the conceptual and symbolic world it represents, linguistic accuracy may obscure more than it reveals. The purpose of Le Guin's paraphrase was to render the Tao Te Ching available rather than precise. Following the same approach, I took each pearl of the Sermon one by one to see if I could give it a poetic polish, burnishing it into something faithful enough to the original to be more Jesus than me, yet startling enough to command the attention of the inured.

What you heard at the outset of this lecture was the end result of that effort. You'll no doubt have noticed exactly where I expanded or even

---

4. I didn't end up repeating "moron" in the final section of the Sermon, because in English the word conveys a kind of frivolous quality that I thought would ring false in the dire conclusion. I stuck with the biblically conventional choice of word, "fool."

5. Lao Tzu, *Tao Te Ching: A Book About the Way and the Power of the Way*, trans. Ursula K. Le Guin (Boston: Shambhala, 1998).

inflated the text in an attempt to capture the range of meaning or accommodate alliteration and assonance; and how in other places I radically trimmed from aphoristic to downright pithy to expose the starkness of a claim: "They ask? You give. They borrow? You lend." I hope the deviations from what you know so well did as intended: forced you to pay attention. For my part, grappling with the Sermon to mold it into a different form did just that.

Alongside my work on the paraphrase, I came at the Sermon from a second angle, in my public role as a preacher. This was back in late 2019 and early 2020 when it was still Matthew year on the lectionary calendar. Those of you who know me well also know how little it takes to set me off about the lectionary, so I apologize in advance, but this is going to be one of those occasions.[6] Run for cover while you can.

Preachers' one shot at most—but not all—of the Sermon on the Mount in sequence falls during the Sundays after Epiphany in Year A.[7] This sequence doesn't begin until the fourth Sunday after Epiphany, however, which will be a real shame in the year 2285 when there only *are* four Sundays after Epiphany at all, Easter being on its earliest possible date that year, namely March 22.

Under normal circumstances, Sundays after Epiphany range from five to seven in number, but the Sermon lections stretch out all the way to the ninth Sunday after Epiphany. We won't enjoy a visitation from that rare bird again during a Matthew year until 2038, when Easter hits its *latest* possible date on April 25. In a reasonably good year like 2023, when Matthew's Gospel next comes round, we'll get a full *seven* Sundays after Epiphany and therefore we'll make it all the way through Matthew chapter 5. But we won't get any of chapter 6, except for an excerpt on Ash Wednesday (which omits the Lord's Prayer and the bits about fasting—gosh, imagine talking about fasting on Ash Wednesday!), and then a little more of chapter 6 many months later, during the Sundays after Pentecost. A portion of Matthew 7 directly follows then, but you won't get it in sequence with the rest of the Sermon until, as I mentioned, 2038,

---

6. For example, Sarah Hinlicky Wilson, "The Top Ten Reasons the Lectionary Sucks and Five Half-Assed Solutions," *Mockingbird*, Apr. 12, 2019; https://mbird.com/2019/04/the-top-ten-reasons-the-lectionary-sucks-and-five-half-assed-solutions/; and Sarah Hinlicky Wilson and Paul Hinlicky, "Taking Another Stab at the Lectionary," *Queen of the Sciences*, Jan. 26, 2021; https://www.queenofthesciences.com/?s=lectionary.

7. There is the traditional reading of the Beatitudes on All Saints' Day, but that is simply the introduction to the Sermon.

and even then you'll only get the latter half of this chapter. I suppose the rationale was that the parallel material in Luke would cover much the same ground. But the fact remains that Matthew 6 and 7 get considerably less time and attention than chapter 5. If you have any instinct whatsoever that the Sermon on the Mount is to be regarded and revered as a distinct unit within the whole Gospel and should be preached accordingly, then you are going to have to gird up your loins and defy the lectionary.

You will not be surprised to hear that I did precisely that in January and February of 2020. The first Sunday I preached on about half of chapter 5, covering the Beatitudes, salt, and light; the next Sunday, the rest of chapter 5; and then one Sunday each for chapter 6 and chapter 7.

And here is where I have to trade out my tone of defiance and irritation for uncertainty and, quite possibly, defeat. On principle I'd say the right thing for a Christian preacher to do is to read and preach on the whole Sermon on the Mount. In practice, I found that I had almost never in my life felt so unequal to a task. This is not false modesty, and if it doesn't sound like terror, it's only because time and distance have lulled me back into my usual false sense of security around the Scriptures.

The core problem of preaching on the Sermon on the Mount turned out to be the simple act of *reading it aloud* to a congregation. This was the most fascinating and troubling aspect of the whole experiment. One advantage of slicing the Sermon up into little lections is that you can control it better that way. You can prevent it from going on too long unchecked before you get your interpretive two cents in. It takes some effort of imagination nowadays to feel how shocking the Beatitudes were: Jesus' homiletic self-introduction was an act of laying blessing upon the least likely persons. But it takes no imagination to feel shocked by announcing *these* lines to the friendly and unsuspecting faces in your pews: "Unless your righteousness exceeds that of the scribes and Pharisees, you will *never* enter the kingdom of heaven." "You will never get out until you have paid the last penny." "If your right hand causes you to sin, cut it off and throw it away. For it is better that you lose one of your members than that your whole body go into hell." As I was reading that last one from the pulpit, I wondered if it was even legal to do so in Japan. Doesn't it count as incitement to violence, even if only against oneself? And do I really have to conclude with "The Gospel of the Lord"?

And these are examples just from chapter 5. It felt disrespectful to tell busy, overworked, exhausted Tokyoites to stop worrying, as I did when reading out chapter 6. Easy for hippie Jesus to say! And then to finish off the whole Sermon with "and great was the fall of that house," with images of Edgar Allan Poe's "The Fall of the House of Usher" dancing in my head . . . By the time I'd finished four weeks of preaching on the Sermon, I felt as if I had been rocked to my core; as if maybe sand was, in fact, preferable to the hardness of the rock I'd been trying to build upon. Uneasy feelings for a preacher to acknowledge!

These two approaches to engaging with the Sermon—a paraphrase as a private poetic and linguistic exercise on the one hand, and public preaching on the other—converged in an unsettling conclusion: I have no idea what the Sermon on the Mount actually *is*. The more time I spend with it, the less I understand it. Even if we could agree on its genre or collection of subgenres, that hardly reduces the burden on the interpreter. The Sermon seems to add up to incalculably more than the sum of its parts.

I am at this point still groping for adequate terminology, but the closest I can come to a single-word descriptor of the Sermon is: Reality. The Sermon on the Mount is Jesus' construction of the hard rock of Reality. Build on it and thrive; defy it and die. Except that it is apparently *not* within one's power to make the choice between rock and sand, as between muffin and cupcake; yet it is also not an option to refuse to make a choice. Action and choice are misleading terms here in any event. The Reality of the Sermon is exposure of the Reality of God, and crashing headlong into the Reality of God results in the exposure of the Reality of Us. A tidy Lutheran doctrinal approach would assign much of the Sermon to the Second Use of the Law, but that doesn't exhaust the matter either, not least of all because I am not sure that I would *want* to run into the arms of the Jesus who preaches this Sermon in order to get relief from the accusations of his Sermon! Is Jesus' crucifixion that which graciously procures my release from this relentless Reality? Or is Jesus' crucifixion the best strategy we've come up with so far for crucifying the Sermon?

It gets worse. The Sermon forces upon me not only uncomfortable self-knowledge, but also uncomfortable other-knowledge. There are hounds that will gobble the holy, pigs that will trample the pearls and then come after me too; the presence of the beam in my eye does not actually invalidate the presence of the twig in my neighbor's; and I need to be on my guard against ravening pseudoprophets in woolly white clothing. There are hypocrites and hordes hastening to destruction. I don't get to relieve myself of the burden of Reality by real or pretended altruism or self-sacrifice. Instead, I am thrown into the sea of sinners and expected to swim. While loving them. Right.

By now, I am tempted to quote the disciples on another occasion—"Who, then, can be saved?"—but I'm not sure I share their goal. The Sermon has left me alarmed by salvation and what it might entail. Possibly Jesus' strategy is to show me all the ways in which I in fact prefer condemnation. And where can I possibly go from there? Gehenna?

Let me turn now to the final act in this inadvertent drama of my existential and homiletic thrashing about. In all my wrangling with the Sermon, I could not but come to my own conclusion about its center—which is undoubtedly wrong, because such a conclusion is an attempt to manage the unmanageable. But if you will be so kind as to take this as a purely provisional handhold, I'll share it with you all the same. This, I sense, is the heart of the Sermon: "The lamp of your life is your eye. So if your eye is laser-focused, your whole being is bright. But if your eye is evil, your whole being is dark. So if the light in you is darkness—**how great the darkness**"

You may have noticed above that I did not add any punctuation to this line, and, as you can see in my duplication of the Greek syntax, it has no verb. It is an exclamation of horror trailing off in the direction of hell: **how great the darkness**

A little prescientific context helps here. The ancients knew there was a connection between light and vision, but they attributed the generation of light to the eye itself, hence "the eye is the lamp of the body." That's what makes the metaphor so chilling. What if the light shed by your eye is actually darkness? Natural darkness is one thing, but spiritual darkness is something else. It's not the opposite of light, but its negation; not light's absence, but its annihilation. What if the very act of looking increases the darkness all around you? Other admonitions in the Sermon warn us against staring at our enemies, at evil: apparently, you become what you look at. That's why you walk the extra mile, jinxing your enemy's evil with an overweening act of generosity. In that way you can still see, if dimly; there's still light. But if your eye is bad, and your light is dark, nothing is going to illumine you again. Natural darkness can be cured with lamplight. But how do you cure darkened light?

At the end of the Sermon, Matthew tells us, the crowds were "astonished" at Jesus' teaching—so the English Standard Version. "Dumbfounded" or "panicked" probably captures the nuance better. And I'm not sure I should do other than leave you similarly panicked. I don't know how to give the Sermon its due without trying to tamp it down again, by a reasonable law, by a gentle grace, by the context of crucifixion, by an eschatology of resurrection. Perhaps for those of us too inured to the symbol of the cross—which once was the final aporia, the inexplicable gulf between imagined and real salvation, between imagined and real divinity—for us, perhaps, the Sermon can, for a moment anyway, take its place: a stumbling block to Jews and a folly to gentiles. "For Christ did not send me to baptize but to preach the Sermon on the Mount, and not with words of eloquent wisdom, lest the Sermon on the Mount be emptied of its power. For the Sermon on the Mount is folly to those who are perishing, but to us who are being saved it is the power of God."

The Gospel of the Lord?

Special Supplement

After the Ball Is Over: The Rise and Decline of the Ecumenical Movement

Michael Root

ONCE UPON A TIME, and a very good time it was, there was a thing called the ecumenical movement.[1] It engaged idealistic men and women across the confessional divides—Protestant, Catholic, and Orthodox—in the quest of greater unity and understanding among divided Christians. Untold hours of work and more money than you might think were poured into these efforts. It attracted public attention; when the National Council of Churches held its inaugural assembly in 1950, the featured speaker was to be no less than the president of the United States (though he did not make it due to snow—perhaps scheduling the assembly for late November in Cleveland wasn't the best idea). When the Presbyterian Eugene Carson Blake in 1960 proposed a union of many mainline Protestant churches, his picture appeared on the cover of *Time* magazine. The early meetings of the US Catholic-Lutheran dialogue ended with honest-to-goodness press conferences, with actual reporters present.

Those days are gone. Public interest has certainly dissolved. I can testify from personal experience with two different publishing houses that the word "ecumenical" is viewed as sales poison. The institutions the ecumenical movement created—councils of churches, denominational ecumenical offices—continue to exist, but they are either on life support, limping along

---

1. This paper was not originally planned as an academic presentation and preserves its more informal character, though notes have been added.

with an ever-decreasing staff, or have turned their interest increasingly to interreligious dialogue and relations, a quite different sort of thing with different motivations and different goals. When a few years ago I taught an undergraduate course on Catholic ecumenism at the Catholic University of America and handed out a survey on the first day on what students would like to learn in the course, one honest student, taking the course because he had to meet the university's theology requirement and this was the only course that fit his schedule, said he hoped to learn what the word "ecumenism" meant (always good to have realistic learning goals, I suppose).

In this presentation I will talk about the ecumenical movement, its rise and decline, and where that leaves those of us still concerned for greater Christian unity. That the ecumenical movement should at some point run out of steam should not be surprising. Perpetual motion machines do not exist; movements at some point stop moving. I have argued in a 2019 essay in *Pro Ecclesia* that we need to attend to various studies from the last century of the nature of large-scale change, which concluded that such change is often not gradual, but comes in large-scale revolutions, which then settle down into relatively stable and enduring patterns, resistant to change, what biologists call "coordinated stasis."[2] The ecumenical movement was a period of significant change; we have now entered, I believe, a period of stability. The question is what to do when the music stops.

The Ecumenical Movement

Let me begin by trying to be more precise about what the phrase "ecumenical movement" refers to. Over the past few decades, social scientists have sought to get a clear sense of what are described as "social movements," with the prime examples being movements for social change—the civil rights movement, the temperance movement, the abolitionist movement. Here is a definition of "social movement" from the second edition of the *International Encyclopedia of the Social Sciences*: "A *social movement* can be defined as a collectivity with mutual awareness in sustained interaction with economic and political elites seeking to forward or halt social change."[3] Let

---

2. Michael Root, "Normal Ecumenism: Ecumenism for the Long Haul," *Pro Ecclesia* 28 (2019) 60–77.

3. Paul Almeida, "Social Movements," in *International Encyclopedia of the Social Sciences*, ed. William A. Darity Jr., 2nd ed. (Detroit: Macmillan Reference USA, 2008), 603–8.

me attempt a slightly more detailed and historically situated definition or brief description of the ecumenical movement, drawing a bit on the social science studies of social movements: The ecumenical movement is (or was) a network of activists and sympathetic supporters from across the spectrum of churches, engaged in sustained and organized activities that sought to move the churches toward greater lived and institutional unity.

A few aspects of this description should be highlighted. First, any movement involves both activists, persons deeply committed to and active in pursuing a goal, and a wider pool of persons who, while more superficially engaged, can be counted on for support at crucial moments. Put crudely, movements require leaders and followers.

Second, movements have goals; they seek to bring about, or to prevent the elimination of, some state of affairs: votes for women, the banning of abortion, the end of slavery. Either something about the current state of affairs is problematic and needs changing; or some good aspect of the current state of affairs is under threat and requires defending. I might add that a factor in the rise of social movements is often a sense that the end sought has become possible. Movements do not long pursue hopeless causes.

Third, movements generally seek to move some institution (institution here used in a broad sense) to change its practices and principles. Movements almost always, at least in their beginnings, involve a certain number of outsiders, that is, persons without influence within the institutions addressed, but often, especially if they are successful, come to include allies within the institutions.

The ecumenical movement of the last century and a quarter fits this description. While a concern for Christian unity had never disappeared in the post-Reformation West, the late nineteenth century saw a gathering momentum. Tracing out causes is difficult, but two crucial developments were the explosion of missionary activity and the shifting demographic and contextual situation for the divided churches. During the late nineteenth century, what some call the Third Great Awakening saw a flood of young men and women into Protestant missions from Britain and America (my great-grandfather among them, a Baptist missionary to what was then Burma). British and American missionaries took with them a burden. We forget that England was close to unique in the European world in the failure of the English Reformation to settle into a single form in a single political unit. It was in England, not the continent, that Protestantism splintered into a variety of churches existing side by side in the same place. Those divisions were exported to America. For many of those recruited into foreign missions in the last decades of the nineteenth century, the difference between Presbyterian, Methodist, Congregationalist, etc., paled in significance before the challenge of converting the Asian and African masses. It is no accident that the first generation of ecumenical leaders tended to come from the missions. For these men and women, I would add, the immediate interest was primarily Protestant unity.

The shifting demographics that I mentioned are harder to pin down, but still visible. In Europe, the loosening bonds between national and confessional identity, the increasing geographical mobility that mixed formerly isolated Catholic and Protestant groups, and the new secular, urban, and industrial environment of life that undercut structures of confessional identity put new pressures on traditional religious boundaries.[4] Political upheavals changed the context for some churches (e.g., the inclusion of large numbers of Catholics under Prussian rule following the Congress of Vienna in 1815 or the impact of the fall of the Russian and Ottoman Empires during and after World War I on the situation of the Orthodox Church).

The ecumenical movement was a popular movement and in its heyday could engage widespread participation. The preparation for the 1957 North American Conference on Faith and Order initially involved small study groups in sixteen cities. Their work produced a pamphlet, *Ecumenical Conversations*, produced as a guide for local conversations. About 350 discussion groups formed, scattered across the country in about forty states. Fifty groups submitted written reports.[5]

And activists increasingly found a receptive ear among church leaders, first among mainstream and established Protestant churches and some Orthodox, then among Catholic leaders following the Second Vatican Council. Despite some naysayers, especially among Evangelical Protestants and conservative Catholics and Orthodox, the ecumenical movement seemed to be moving from success to success in the 1950s and 1960s.

---

4. On the complex ways these larger social trends interacted with confessional identity in Germany, see the essays in Helmut Walser Smith, ed., *Protestants, Catholics, and Jews in Germany, 1800-1914* (Oxford: Berg, 2001).

5. Paul S. Minear, "The Conference in Context," *The Nature of the Unity We Seek: Official Report of the North American Conference on Faith and Order, September 3-10, 1957, Oberlin, Ohio*, ed. Paul S. Minear (St. Louis: Bethany, 1958), 11-27, at 16-17.

Problems and Decline

What Is Being Sought?

Yet, there were problems from the start. As I noted, any social movement seeks some sort of goal, a change it wants to bring about or halt. The ecumenical movement sought greater unity among Christians. But what sort of unity? That question dogged the ecumenical movement almost from the start and created a deep problem, in perhaps two ways.

First, how is unity to be defined theologically and organizationally? Is unity defined as a common definable creedal statement? Does it involve shared communion? Need there be a commonly recognized ordained ministry? Need there be shared structures of common and binding decision making? These questions were particularly problematic because they involved fundamental issues of ecclesiology that were themselves disputed between the churches. In a sense, to agree on the ecumenical goal was to agree on the nature of the church, and disagreement on the nature of the church was one of the primary obstacles to reaching the goal. I have sometimes thought that we will reach agreement on the ecumenical goal only when the goal has been achieved.

The concrete form this question took was whether the ecumenical goal was some sort of fellowship or communion of essentially independent churches or some organically unified body, something more like the individual churches as they now exist. A complicating factor requiring more study, I believe, is the change in the structure of the individual churches in the late nineteenth and early twentieth centuries. Crudely stated, during that period, national churches moved from being networks that came together periodically, both regionally and nationally, for particular purposes toward being large bureaucracies administering an array of programs.[6] In this new situation, "organic unity," the sense of unity preferred by many early ecumenical leaders, inevitably took on the features of a merger of bureaucracies.

In the English-speaking world—the US, Britain, Anglophone Africa, India—the pursuit of organic unity was the reef on which ecumenism in its initial form, the pursuit of Protestant unity, ran aground. We forget today the enormous effort poured into the proposed merger of much of American mainline Protestantism in the 1960s and 1970s through the

---

6. Russell E. Richey, "Denominationalism," in *Encyclopedia of Religion in America*, ed. Charles H. Lippy and Peter W. Williams (Washington, DC: CQ Press, 2010), 1:544–46.

Consultation on Church Union, only to have the proposed plan of union fail to be accepted by the churches.[7] The same experience was replicated in other countries, with similar results (with the exception of the successful union plans of the Indian subcontinent). In the wake of these disappointments, Protestant churches turned in the 1970s and 1980s to various models of "full communion," in which the churches remained organizationally distinct, while sharing ministries and sacraments. (Lutherans had always favored such an understanding of unity.) Even for those who worked hard for these proposals (and few worked harder than I did on the Episcopal-Lutheran proposal in this country), the results have been underwhelming. The churches cooperate on the margins, but for the most part life goes on unchanged. The ecumenical movement failed to define a goal that was achievable and significant. Joseph Small has raised the question whether what has been achieved can rightly be called "full communion."[8] By many standards, the answer must be no.

But there was a second, more underground problem related to the ecumenical goal. What did the proverbial person in the pew who supported some sort of greater Christian unity, but could not be called an activist, actually want? What was the itch that sought scratching? In preparation for the 1957 North American Conference on Faith and Order, five thousand laity and clergy were surveyed on their attitudes to Christian unity. Strikingly, less than 10 percent supported some form of organizational unity. About 90 percent rejected the idea that Christian unity meant "the gathering of all Christians into one visible church organization."[9] The failure of COCU was perhaps predictable; it sought a goal few wanted.

But let me press the question further and in an admittedly speculative way. The twentieth century saw in the United States a profound shift in patterns of church membership. The Princeton sociologist Robert Wuthnow notes data indicating that in 1955 only one in twenty-five Americans had changed denominations during their lifetime, while in 1985 about one

---

7. Keith Watkins, *The American Church That Might Have Been: A History of the Consultation on Church Union* (Eugene, OR: Pickwick, 2014).

8. Joseph D. Small, "What Is Communion and When Is It Full?" *Ecclesiology* 2 (2005) 71–87.

9. Walter G. Muelder, "Institutionalism in Relation to Unity and Diversity," in *The Nature of the Unity We Seek: Official Report of the North American Conference on Faith and Order, September 3–10, 1957, Oberlin, Ohio*, ed. Paul S. Minear (St. Louis: Bethany, 1958), 90–102, at 92.

third had.[10] A Pew Research Center study of 2008 found that 44 percent of Americans identified their present religious affiliation as different than that in which they had grown up, with over a quarter having shifted one major tradition to another (i.e., not from one Protestant church to another Protestant church).[11] More than a quarter of adults surveyed were in religiously mixed marriages (not counting spouses in two different Protestant churches).[12] There have also been profound changes in religious attitudes. A 2017 Pew study indicated that more than half of both Protestants and Catholics in the US believe that Catholics and Protestants are more alike than different.[13] A similar survey of Western Europe found similar results.[14] Comparative data for the past is not available, but it is hard to imagine that such attitudes were widespread in nineteenth-century America or Europe. The data shows that this shift is related to a low level of commitment to the doctrines that have historically split the churches. The Pew survey found that only 30 percent of American Protestants accepted both "Scripture alone" and "salvation by faith alone," a smaller percentage than those who said they accepted neither.[15] (One can argue about the way the survey phrased its questions, but the result is still striking.)

Finally, changes in worship practices have made crossing religious boundaries, occasionally or regularly, less alienating. The liturgical movement has influenced most churches. Vestments have become more common and uniform; the liturgical calendar more widely used. The Catholic Mass is no longer in Latin.

Taken together, these changes mean that moving about among churches is now less alienating, less uncomfortable, less confusing. A son or a daughter marrying a person of another church is less upsetting, more expected. And Americans have taken advantage of this shift; they have moved among

---

10. Robert Wuthnow, *The Restructuring of American Religion: Society and Faith Since World War II* (Princeton, NJ: Princeton University Press, 1988), 88–89.

11. Pew Research Center, *U.S. Religious Landscape Survey: Religious Affiliation: Diverse and Dynamic* (Washington, DC: Pew Forum on Religion & Public Life, 2008), 22.

12. Pew Research Center, *U.S. Religious Landscape Survey*, 34–35.

13. Pew Research Center, *U.S. Protestants Are Not Defined by Reformation-Era Controversies 500 Years Later* (Washington, DC: Pew Forum on Religion & Public Life, 2017), 22.

14. Pew Research Center, *Five Centuries After Reformation, Catholic-Protestant Divide in Western Europe Has Faded* (Washington, DC: Pew Forum on Religion & Public Life, 2017), 4.

15. Pew Research Center, *U.S. Protestants*, 5.

churches. Did the ecumenical movement run out of steam because church division had become, for the average person in the pew, painless, perfectly comfortable? The itch that needed scratching had disappeared.

Let me press the point a speculative step further. Is the present situation among the churches, which can be described as friendly division with porous borders, the religious condition that fits best with a culture shaped by mass market consumer capitalism? Contemporary capitalism runs on catering to the slightest nuance of consumer choice. Do you want your orange juice with no pulp, some pulp, or "most pulp," as I saw recently? And consumer choice is celebrated as a way to express who you are. Do you want a special sort of Oreos to celebrate Pride Month, Oreos with rainbow-shaded filling? You can find them (at least, you can find them talked about on the internet). Within this structure, we function as forms of desire to be catered to and shaped by an endless and changing flow of enticing offers, the more and the more distinct, the better. We don't want literal cola wars; we don't want Coke and Pepsi to literally firebomb each others' facilities, but we want them to remain different. After all, sometimes you feel like a nut, sometimes you don't, as the ad for Mounds and Almond Joy used to say. In this context, Presbyterian and Catholic become the equivalent of Jiff and Skippy. We need to face the question whether friendly division with porous borders is the form of church life that results from the deeply formative powers of our consumer-oriented economic culture.

The Present Limits of Agreement

Another set of issues has also I believe contributed to the ecumenical movement running out of steam. So far, I have focused primarily on one strand of the ecumenical movement, the drive toward Protestant unity. As that impetus was reaching its peak, another ecumenical avenue opened up: Protestant-Catholic dialogue in the wake of the Second Vatican Council. For many involved in the Center for Catholic and Evangelical Theology, this avenue was the most exciting side of ecumenism and the one that offered the greatest possibility for theological and ecclesial renewal. Ecumenism here took a different form. There was still engagement at the local level; the Living Room Dialogues, a program of the 1960s to bring together Protestants, Catholics, and Orthodox at the local level for discussion, was a success.[16] But two factors were different than the earlier

16. William A. Norgren, *Faith and Order in the U.S.A.: A Brief History of Studies and*

ecumenical developments. On the one hand, the traditionally divisive theological issues—the papacy, devotion to the Virgin Mary, doctrines and practices surrounding the Mass—were both more obviously still seen as divisive and more visibly present in daily religious life. These issues would need to be addressed in detail before significant steps toward unity would be possible, and that meant that dialogues involving trained theologians would have to play a greater role than in intra-Protestant and conciliar ecumenism. On the other, the worldwide and more centralized character of the organization of the Catholic Church meant that decisions that could dismantle barriers to communion would need to be ratified by the worldwide church, which concretely meant ratified by Rome. International dialogues thus took on a structural importance.

Rome cannot be faulted for lack of institutional effort. The Catholic Church still carries out the widest range of ecumenical dialogues of any church body. And the early years of dialogue, especially with Anglicans and Lutherans, showed great promise. In retrospect, one can see that the successes came mostly in topics related to the nature of salvation and its mediation—justification and grace, the sacraments. The 1999 Catholic-Lutheran *Joint Declaration on the Doctrine of Justification* was the great achievement of this side of the dialogues.[17]

The dialogues ran into a wall, however. When dialogues turned to concrete questions of how we live out the faith as a community, that is, when they turned to the church and its way of life, agreement became difficult beyond highly general statements. The issue is not just the papacy, but the role of the bishop in the diocese and the priest in the parish. Nor can these issues be avoided. Church unity, the Catholic Church has held, requires unity in teaching, sacraments, and governance.[18] Some form of common decision-making and discipline is an essential aspect of the unity of the church, and the details—Who makes the decisions on what topics? Who carries out discipline?—are nontrivial for the actual life of the church. Such questions are much harder to finesse by the conceptual strategies the dialogues used to defuse some traditional doctrinal issues. For example, dialogues have often sought to reframe an issue in different

---

Relationships (Grand Rapids: Eerdmans, 2011), 25–26.

17. The Lutheran World Federation and the Roman Catholic Church, *Joint Declaration on the Doctrine of Justification* (Grand Rapids: Eerdmans, 2000).

18. See, e.g., Vatican II's decree on ecumenism, *Unitatis Redintegratio*, §2; in Norman P. Tanner, ed., *Decrees of the Ecumenical Councils* (London: Sheed & Ward, 1990), 2:909.

categories, categories in which an old problem can be stated in a different and more tractable way. But when discussion comes to papal authority, the necessity of episcopal order, or the ordination of women, however the issue is framed, the concrete question reappears: Will the bishop of Rome remain the court of last appeal within the church? Must a church have an episcopal order? Will or can the church ordain women? Finding a middle ground becomes far more difficult.

The temptation is to say that this blockage in the area of ecclesiology is itself a sign of corruption, of a self-regarding bureaucracy holding the Spirit hostage. That view is, I believe, profoundly false. Ecumenism, in the end, is not about the relation between ideas nor about the relation between professors in a dialogue. It is about the relation between concrete communities. How do they find a life together in Christ? The lives of these communities are structured by fundamental commitments, some of which are historically conditioned and dispensable, some of which are simply sinful. Some, however, express convictions that are believed to be rooted in the gospel. Concrete issues of practice can help us see where the decisive issues are and can guide ecumenical theology. It is a topic that would take us too far afield, but I believe the differences in ecclesiology that separate Protestants and Catholics are tied up with unresolved issues about how grace engages both the individual Christian and the church (issues about grace that did not arise in the *Joint Declaration on the Doctrine of Justification* because they relate to justification in oblique ways).

An additional factor in the present situation needs to be added. While the problems that led to past divisions were being addressed by the dialogues, the churches did not remain unchanged. At the time of the Second Vatican Council, disagreements over ethics between Catholic and most Protestant churches were minor. Over the last few decades, however, sharp differences have arisen between mainline Protestant churches on the one hand and the Catholic, Orthodox, and Evangelical churches on the other hand over a cluster of issues relating to sex and sexuality, most notably, abortion and same-sex relations. The few ecumenical dialogues that have taken up these recent ethical divergences have done little more than register the impasse.[19] While these issues may not be fundamental within the hier-

---

19. See Roman Catholic and United Church of Canada, *Marriage: Report of the Roman Catholic/United Church Dialogue, October 2004—April 2012*, Ecumenism, May 16, 2012; https://ecumenism.net/archive/dialogues_ca/2012_rc_ucc_marriage_en.pdf; and Anglican-Roman Catholic Theological Consultation in the U.S.A., "Ecclesiology and Moral Discernment: Seeking a Unified Moral Witness," USCCB, Apr. 22, 2014; https://

archy of truths abstractly considered, they are immediately understandable and relevant to the average Christian in a way that differences over, say, justification and grace are not. A significant portion of typical churchgoers in Catholic, mainline Protestant, Orthodox, and Evangelical churches have firm convictions on these issues. They will not go away soon. If anything, their importance should be expected to grow.

These sharp divides over ethical and more generally gender-related issues have not simply been between the churches, of course, but also within the churches. One might think this would bring churches together as they seek common strategies of reconciliation, but that has not been the case. In general, churches undergoing intense internal strains have difficulty pursuing ecumenical goals. Often, in these internal debates the question arises of who is being "truly Reformed," or "truly Anglican," or "truly Catholic." The specificities (and thus the differentia) of the differing traditions have a tendency to get highlighted.

I mentioned earlier that studies of social movements often note that movements arise when change (or the prevention of change) seems possible. The state of theology in the early twentieth century contained within it possibilities of reconciliation on a range of what can be called soteriological issues, issues related to salvation. The possibilities of agreement on those topics have now been realized. On other topics, ecclesiology and ethics especially, the present state of doctrine and theological conviction in our churches seems to rule out the sort of agreement needed for church communion, at least in the foreseeable future. As a result, ecumenical dialogues, where they continue, mostly spin their wheels and, I believe, will continue to do so if they continue along the lines laid out in the 1960s and 1970s.

Ecumenism and Renewal

I could go on; I could say something about the way the organizations created by the ecumenical movement, e.g., the World Council of Churches and, in the US, the National Council of Churches, evolved into institutions increasingly dominated by their own bureaucracies, cut off from many of the member churches, and increasingly irrelevant. I do want to add one more comment, though it is hard to verify. I want to mention it because I think it is perhaps decisive for the deep shift in interest in ecumenical matters both among clergy and theologians and within the wider church.

---

www.usccb.org/resources/arcusa-2014-statement.pdf.

The ecumenical movement, in its origins and at least through the 1980s, was seen by many as a renewal movement. A more united church would be a richer, more faithful church, a church more evangelical and more catholic, a more vital church. I can speak from my own experience (with the attendant risk, I grant, that I am projecting my experience onto others). My own ecumenical engagement was initially sparked, not by an abstract theological commitment to unity, but by what I read and learned in the mid-1970s in George Lindbeck's class on ecumenical dialogues. Ecumenism seemed to promise a deeper, fuller version of my own Lutheran tradition and, I trusted, a richer, fuller version of the Reformed and Catholic and other traditions. My sense of the commitments of my mentors—Lindbeck, Robert Jenson, William Rusch—and of those I read with appreciation—Catholics such as Otto-Hermann Pesch and Yves Congar, Methodists such as Geoffrey Wainwright, Reformed such as Lesslie Newbigin—was that they too were moved by the sense that ecumenism meant renewal.

A fundamental reason for a widespread disinterest in matters ecumenical among clergy, laity, and theologians is, I believe, the waning or disappearance of a sense that the ecumenism is a likely source of renewal or enrichment. Ecumenical events, ecumenical texts, ecumenical proposals, ecumenical institutions may have their virtues, but they are no longer widely perceived as sources of a richer, deeper church life. Perhaps this development is simply the inevitable evolution of the ecumenical movement from charisma to institution. Perhaps it is partially the result of the adoption of ecumenical proposals without any real change in church life. Perhaps it is was the fault of the ecumenical professionals (such as myself). While I do not know of survey data that would back up this perception, my sense is that "ecumenism as renewal" ceased for most to be convincing.

Ecumenism After the Ecumenical Movement

By now will you have probably gotten my point. I believe the ecumenical movement has run its course. It has accomplished what it is going to accomplish.

But you may be wondering, why am I insisting on this point with such emphasis? Am I protesting a bit too much? Is there an agenda behind my argument, an axe being ground in the background? Well, yes, to a degree there is.

I believe that continuing to press forward along the path laid out by the twentieth-century ecumenical movement, using the tools and methods developed by that movement, is counterproductive; it makes a fuller realization of the unity now possible more difficult. A problem for contemporary ecumenism is an addiction to progress, understood as official agreements that represent incremental progress toward unity. Since the ecumenical agreements at the end of the last century—the *Joint Declaration on the Doctrine of Justification* and the wave of intra-Protestant full communion agreements—few such official agreements have been proposed (mostly, I believe, because further agreements that would justify such proposals have not proven plausible). The temptation is to allow the will to unity to substitute for agreement and to insist on intercommunion between Catholics and Protestants on the basis of what has been achieved. A prime example of this push is the recent statement of the German Ecumenical Study Group, *Together at the Lord's Table*,[20] a proposal being seriously considered in the German Catholic "Synodal Way," despite strong criticism by the Vatican.

For Catholic theology (and for much Protestant theology prior to the twentieth century), intercommunion without full unity is theologically problematic. The reception of the Eucharist is both a sign and a realization of full communion with the community here and around the world (and thus every Catholic Mass states its unity with the local bishop and the pope).

There are also practical ecumenical concerns. The experience of the full communion agreements of the last twenty years I think indicates that intercommunion generally stalls movement toward greater unity and tacitly plays into the hand of an understanding of the churches as options of consumer choice.

The question about intercommunion is sometimes phrased as a question about what is necessary as a precondition for eucharistic sharing. I think the question is better put as a question about what must follow eucharistic sharing. Can we rightly share in the Eucharist if we are not going to lead a genuinely common ecclesial life afterward? In the 1980s, long before I was received in the Catholic Church, I came to the conclusion that eucharistic sharing without a following common life was inappropriate and so did not receive communion when a common life was not possible.

---

20. Dorothea Sattler and Volker Leppin, eds., *Gemeinsam am Tisch des Herrn: Ein Votum des ökumenischen Arbeitskreises evangelischer und katholischer Theologen—Together at the Lord's Table: A Statement of the Ecumenical Study Group of Protestant and Catholic Theologians*, Dialog der Kirchen 17 (Freiburg: Herder, 2020).

The question may be crossing your mind, quite rightly, whether what I am delivering is a counsel of despair and perhaps even an abandonment of the virtue of hope in relation to Christian unity. If the ecumenical movement is over, is ecumenism over? Is it time to pack our ecumenical bags and go home? The answer has to be an emphatic no. The waning of the ecumenical movement must not mean that concerns for Christian unity should now die. Christians remain divided, and that is no less a scandal today than it was in 1920 or 1600 or 1300 or 700. There may be limits to what can be done about that scandal at the moment. People of good faith can and do disagree on fundamental matters, and disagreement among Christians on some important matters goes back to the New Testament (read the letters of Paul or the letters of John). But it is also true that we (or at least I) fall into sin repeatedly and all too predictably, yet I am still called to resist sin and seek to grow in grace. We are called to seek what unity across confessional divides is possible, even if such unity is less than perfect.

But, you ask, what do we do? Let me say first and with some emphasis that the first ecumenical task remains what it always was, the task of internal conversion, which is the task of conformity to Christ. "Have this mind among you, which is yours in Christ Jesus," Paul exhorts the Philippians before launching into the great Christological hymn of chapter 2. We can agree—Catholic, Orthodox, and Protestants—that the task of conforming us to Christ is above all the task of the Holy Spirit at work within us. But we also agree that we are ourselves to seek to curb the old Adam and Eve within ourselves and cooperate with the Spirit in that work.

American culture at the moment seems to have lost the sense that it is possible to recognize both agreement on decisive fundamentals and disagreement on matters of lesser, though still significant, importance. Yes, the devil is at work in the world, but those who disagree with us are not necessarily the devil's minions. A great mistake of many on both sides of the Reformation divides was their blindness to the possibility of disagreement in good faith. Today the spiritual challenge, the challenge to our souls, is not presented by the relation between what might be called the conservative Lutheran and the conservative Catholic, but between, say, the conservative Evangelical and the liberal Episcopalian. Can they recognize their unity in baptism, while also recognizing the sharp differences on a series of neuralgic issues? In that context, how do we have the mind of Christ among us?

In action, the challenge is to find ways that maintain, strengthen, and witness to our unity, despite division. Let me focus briefly on two areas.

First, activities at the local or regional level need to find ways to continue. I have little concrete to say on this topic, and what I can say does not come out of any expertise. I am, after all, a theology professor and a layman, professionally impractical, one might say. I don't pass over this topic in silence because I want to note its importance and how difficult the task in this area is. I am willing to be corrected, even desire to be corrected, but my observation is that at the local and regional level, looking beyond the congregation/parish or the diocese/synod/presbytery still takes effort. Life within the individual Protestant congregations, especially on the more Evangelical wing, is less determined than in the past by denominational education materials and hymnbooks, but that does not mean that their life is particularly ecumenical. One thing I believe we have learned from a century of ecumenical efforts is how resilient traditional structures are; they may change in unpredictable ways, but they remain in place.

I have more to say on a second topic, the theological encounter of the traditions. For better or worse, the bilateral "dialogue of experts," as it was put, became the ecumenical method that attracted most attention in the last quarter of the twentieth century. I have noted their real but limited success and their present exhaustion. They still go on, although mostly unnoticed, with reduced funding, less frequent meetings, and lowered expectations. On the more intractable topics they now face, dialogues are forced to remain at a high level of generality in order to stress agreement. The results are not just thin, but worse, often boring. How many attending this conference (or reading this essay) have actually read a recent statement from an ecumenical dialogue?

One solution to this impasse is what is called "receptive ecumenism," a term invented and popularized in Britain. Receptive ecumenism would not focus on the pursuit of an agreement that probably is unreachable. Rather, the participating traditions each seek what they can learn from the other tradition, in particular what they can learn in relation to their own weaknesses. The international Anglican-Catholic dialogue has adopted "receptive ecumenism" as a strategy.[21]

I believe more important is finding ways for theologians of different traditions to engage across confessional traditions in less formal, less official settings. Such engagements can be in person (such as these conferences

---

21. Paul D. Murray, "In Search of a Way," in *The Oxford Handbook of Ecumenical Studies*, ed. Geoffrey Wainwright and Paul McPartlan (New York: Oxford University Press, 2021), 613–29.

or the activities of the Chicago Theological Initiative) or online, though I have found few such online discussions. Such unofficial events need to find ways to engage those doubtful about ecumenism as they have experienced it. Most importantly, they must be interesting and engaging.

    I will stop here because, in fact, I don't have a program for the future. I can't say with any confidence "do this" or "do that." What I can say is that I think the old methods and old programs have long since done what good they can. Those of us committed to addressing in some way the division of Christians must find new forms of engagement, a post–ecumenical movement ecumenism. Whatever the new forms might be, we need to proceed with a clear sense of what our present situation is, its possibilities, and its limitations. Blind action, I believe, will at the present moment make matters worse, not better.

www.ingramcontent.com/pod-product-compliance
Lightning Source LLC
Chambersburg PA
CBHW032235080426
42735CB00008B/865